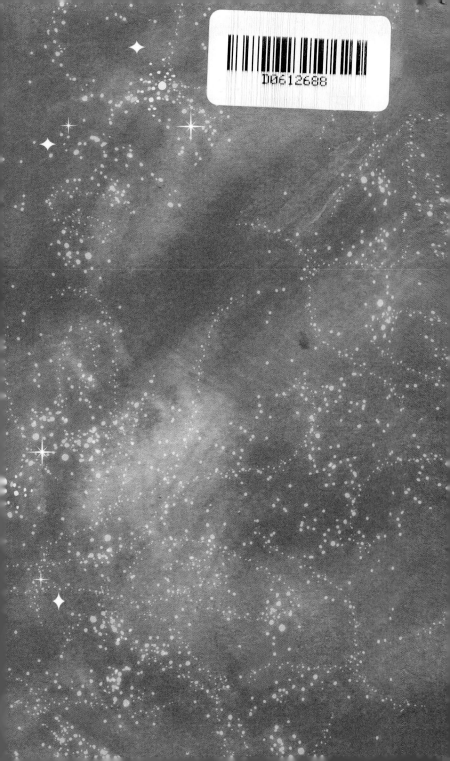

THE
ASTROLOGY
COMPANION

· · · · ● ● · · · ·

The Portable Guide for
Using the Planets to Manifest
Your Power and Purpose

TANAAZ CHUBB

FAIR WINDS

Inspiring | Educating | Creating | Entertaining

Brimming with creative inspiration, how-to projects, and useful information to enrich your everyday life, quarto.com is a favorite destination for those pursuing their interests and passions.

© 2022 Quarto Publishing Group USA Inc.
Text © 2021 Tanaaz Chubb

First Published in 2022 by Fair Winds Press, an imprint of The Quarto Group,
100 Cummings Center, Suite 265-D, Beverly, MA 01915, USA.
T (978) 282-9590 F (978) 283-2742 Quarto.com

Fair Winds Press titles are also available at discount for retail, wholesale, promotional, and bulk purchase. For details, contact the Special Sales Manager by email at specialsales@quarto.com or by mail at The Quarto Group, Attn: Special Sales Manager, 100 Cummings Center, Suite 265-D, Beverly, MA 01915, USA.

25 24 23 22   1 2 3 4 5

ISBN: 978-0-7603-7793-2

Digital edition published in 2022
eISBN: 978-1-58923-988-3

The content in this book appeared in the previously published book *The Ultimate Guide to Astrology* (Fair Winds Press 2021) by Tanaaz Chubb.

Originally found under the following Library of Congress Cataloging-in-Publication Data
Names: Chubb, Tanaaz, author.
Title: The ultimate guide to astrology: use the guidance of the planets to manifest your power and purpose / Tanaaz Chubb.
Description: Beverly : Fair Winds Press, 2021. | Series: The ultimate guide to... | Includes index. | Summary: "With The Ultimate Guide to Astrology, leading astrologer and Instagram star Tanaaz Chubb presents a modern and accessible approach to astrology with an emphasis on the signs and the planets"-- Provided by publisher.
Identifiers: LCCN 2020052521 (print) | LCCN 2020052522 (ebook) | ISBN 9781589239876 (trade paperback) | ISBN 9781589239883 (ebook)
Subjects: LCSH: Astrology. | Astrology and vocational guidance.
Classification: LCC BF1708.1 .C48 2021 (print) | LCC BF1708.1 (ebook) | DDC 133.5--dc23
LC record available at https://lccn.loc.gov/2020052521
LC ebook record available at https://lccn.loc.gov/2020052522

Design: Allison Meierding
Page Layout: Allison Meierding
Illustration: Suzanne Washington

Printed in China

DEDICATION

Dedicated to my dear friend, Rachel,
who first introduced me to the magic of astrology.

CONTENTS

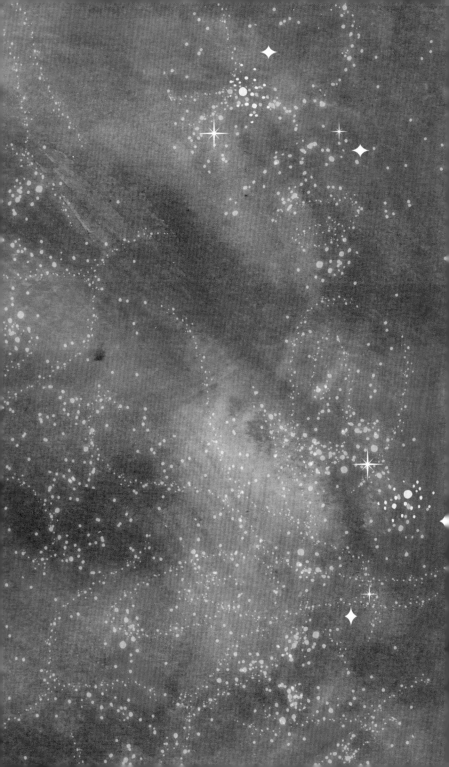

INTRODUCTION

Astrology is the study of our connection to the cosmos. At the moment you were born, the planets and stars aligned in a configuration that holds the energetic blueprint of your soul and the energetic forces that surround you.

I was first introduced to astrology by my friend Rachel. Through the years, it has helped me peel back the layers to reveal new truths and insights about myself. Astrology gently guides you to understand the energetic frequencies that you can harness to lead a balanced, connected, and richer life. It can also highlight some lessons your soul has come to learn, and why certain vibrations or themes may be present.

This book will break down the basic components of astrology and set you on the path to reading and understanding the vibrations that surround you and the messages they hold. Get ready to connect with the cosmic skies, the cosmic blueprint of your soul, and the foundation of the ancient art of astrology. Enjoy the journey!

Section 1

• • • • • • • •

YOUR MAP TO THE COSMIC SKIES

Astrology connects the Universe around you to the Universe within you. It uses a formula or chart system to help make sense of the planets, the zodiac signs, and the energies they are creating. Once you understand the basics, you will be able to read your own chart, the charts of others, and the chart of our present time.

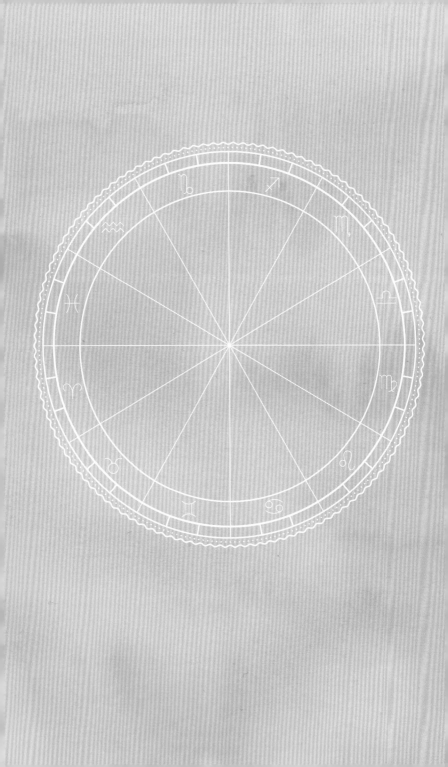

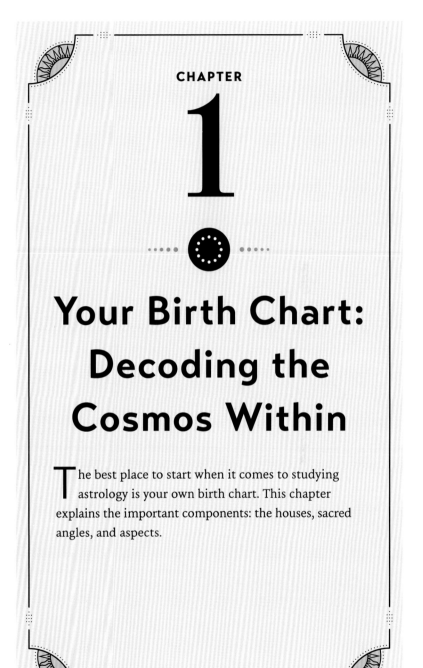

1

Your Birth Chart: Decoding the Cosmos Within

The best place to start when it comes to studying astrology is your own birth chart. This chapter explains the important components: the houses, sacred angles, and aspects.

HOUSES

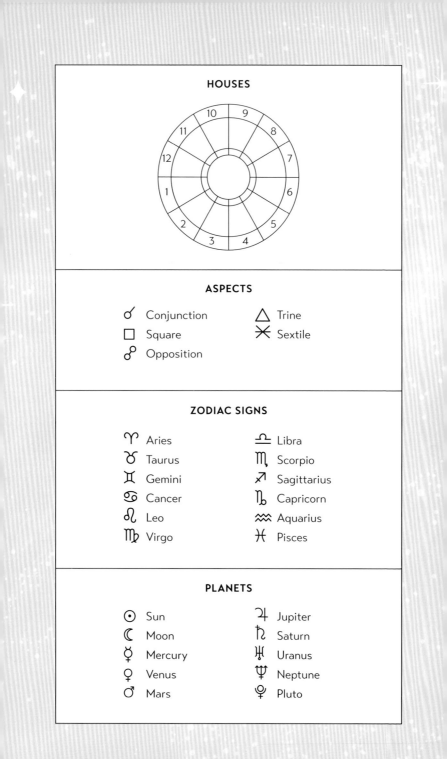

ASPECTS

☌	Conjunction	△	Trine
□	Square	✳	Sextile
☍	Opposition		

ZODIAC SIGNS

♈	Aries	♎	Libra
♉	Taurus	♏	Scorpio
♊	Gemini	♐	Sagittarius
♋	Cancer	♑	Capricorn
♌	Leo	♒	Aquarius
♍	Virgo	♓	Pisces

PLANETS

☉	Sun	♃	Jupiter
☽	Moon	♄	Saturn
☿	Mercury	♅	Uranus
♀	Venus	♆	Neptune
♂	Mars	♇	Pluto

DRAWING AND
DECODING YOUR CHART

There are many free online tools that will draw your birth chart. I recommend printing a copy so it's easier to follow along.

For the most accurate birth chart, you will need to know your exact time of birth. If you don't know the exact time, draw your chart with the time set to 12 p.m. The house placements will not be accurate, so you won't be able to determine your rising sign or other sacred angles. Nevertheless, you can build a great snapshot of the energies you are working with.

HOUSES

In Western astrology, your chart is drawn as a 360-degree wheel divided into twelve sections, or houses. Each house represents a different area of your life and your soul journey.

Each house is associated with one of the twelve zodiac signs. You have your own astrological signs for each house, making your chart unique! The planets are sprinkled through your chart based on where they were at the time of your birth.

Because each house carries a particular theme, the zodiac sign and any planets within that house can indicate where you are likely to see the energy manifesting the most in your life. For example, the tenth house rules over your career, so any planet in this part of the chart is likely to express itself in your work or public life.

THE THEMES OF EACH HOUSE

House	Natural Rulers	Themes
FIRST HOUSE: I AM	*Aries and the planet Mars*	Self, ego, your identity, your personality, your body, general temperament, early childhood, approach to life, physical health, vitality
SECOND HOUSE: I POSSESS	*Taurus and the planet Venus*	Earned income, self-worth, material possessions, values, sense of security, confidence
THIRD HOUSE: I EXPRESS	*Gemini and the planet Mercury*	Self-expression, mind, intellect, speaking, communication, siblings/cousins, domestic travel, coworkers, local neighborhood, perception of childhood, adaptability
FOURTH HOUSE: I BELONG	*Cancer and the Moon*	Home and family life, property, who you are when no one is watching, real estate, domestic life, parents, later life, ancestry, private life, endings
FIFTH HOUSE: I CREATE	*Leo and the Sun*	Creativity, children, romance, fun, pleasure, dating, artistic abilities, hobbies, recreational activities, gambling, pregnancy
SIXTH HOUSE: I HEAL	*Virgo and the planet Mercury*	General health, productivity, your day-to-day routine, animals, duties, diet, fitness, energy level, workplace environment
SEVENTH HOUSE: I CONNECT	*Libra and the planet Venus*	Relationships, how you relate to others, people you are in business with, contracts, contractual relationships, marriage, divorce, conflicts

EIGHTH HOUSE: I TRANSFORM	Scorpio and the planet Pluto	Transformation, investments, inheritance, taxes, insurance, death and rebirth, the taboo, sex, drugs/alcohol, psychic, occult, sleep, surgery, joint finances, investigation, research
NINTH HOUSE: I SEEK	Sagittarius and the planet Jupiter	Learning, teaching, higher education, higher mind, philosophy, publishing, justice, legal issues, international travel, humanitarian efforts, grandchildren, in-laws, law, ethics
TENTH HOUSE: I PURSUE	Capricorn and the planet Saturn	Career, fame, public persona, purpose, reputation, status, ambitions, employer, government, desire for power, success, professional life
ELEVENTH HOUSE: I DREAM	Aquarius and the planet Uranus	Friendships, community, groups or clubs, religion, hopes, dreams and wishes, technology, humanitarianism, group thinking, large social events, networking
TWELFTH HOUSE: I TRANSCEND	Pisces and the planet Neptune	Secrets, struggles, the unconscious, behind-the-scenes, shadow self, psychic gifts, karma, jails, hospitals, subconscious mind, intuition, healing, confinement, self-sabotage, escapism

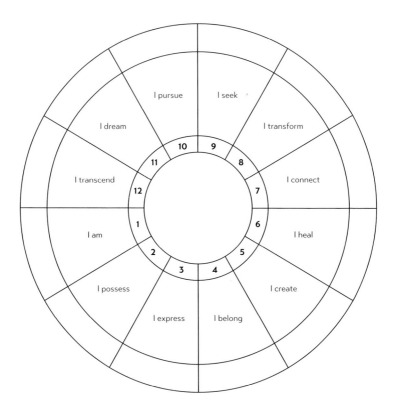

EMPTY HOUSES

If a house is empty, check which zodiac sign rules over that house in your own chart to see what qualities would be most active in that part of your life. For example, if Gemini is the ruler of your tenth house, when it comes to your career, you may find yourself tapping into the gift of communication that Gemini can bring.

SACRED ANGLES

The twelve houses of your chart are all important; however, there are four angles that carry extra significance. These four angles are each ruled by a sign of the zodiac.

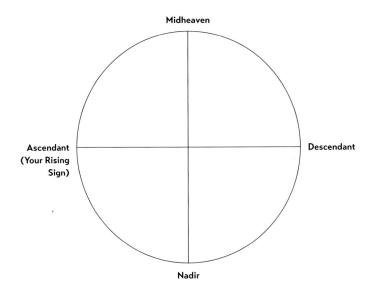

The Ascendant or Rising Sign

The ascendant, or rising sign, is located between the twelfth and first house. It is the zodiac that was on the horizon at the time of your birth. Think of your rising sign as the starting point to your entire chart. Your rising sign represents the "outer" you, the person you are before someone gets to know you.

YOUR RISING SIGN

Rising Sign	Ruled By	Meaning
Aries	*Mars*	You appear confident, courageous, and bold. You are a headstrong go-getter, and you love to do things your own way. Be mindful of overcommitting yourself. It's okay to release control and ask for help when you need it.
Taurus	*Venus*	You are down-to-earth and easygoing, but there is a lot going on beneath the surface. You are loyal and responsible, and people tend to trust you easily.
Gemini	*Mercury*	You are friendly and seem to get along well with everyone. You are good at adapting to any situation. Make sure you aren't sacrificing too much of yourself to fit in.
Cancer	*The Moon*	You are sensitive and caring but also fiercely loyal and protective. You do all you can to look after what you care about. You have a strong intuition, so be sure to listen to its wisdom.
Leo	*The Sun*	You have a fun-loving energy, and you tend to thrive when you are in the spotlight and when you feel passionate about something. Vibrant and warm, you have a creative spark that shines through your eyes.
Virgo	*Mercury*	You are practical and well organized, and you know how to keep your composure no matter what. A natural caregiver, you are compassionate and considerate. Make sure you treat yourself with the same loving-kindness that you so easily show to others.
Libra	*Venus*	You have a way of making everyone around you feel comfortable. You seem to know what others need and are in tune with your environment. Your keen insights make you a great people person, and you can soothe tensions and find the middle ground. Make sure you don't lose sight of yourself in your efforts to support others.

Scorpio	*Pluto*	You draw people in with your highly magnetic and attractive energy. You may come across as secretive or a little mysterious, and this is because you have many complex layers. You and those you let in will never be bored, for you are always traveling deeper and looking to understand yourself from new depths.
Sagittarius	*Jupiter*	People are drawn to your sunny personality and your playful and carefree attitude. You have the gift of seeing the lighter side of life. By embracing this, you can remain cool, calm, and collected in the midst of chaos. You are always searching for adventure; just don't forget to balance your responsibilities as well.
Capricorn	*Saturn*	You can appear a little serious and maybe even closed off, but when people get to know you, your witty sense of humor, intelligence, and warm personality shine through. You are hardworking, responsible, highly motivated, and ambitious when you put your mind to something.
Aquarius	*Uranus*	You do things in your own way. You love sharing your wisdom, resources, and ideas, and you are always willing to lend a hand. Although you are friendly to all, you are a private person, and it can take a while before you feel comfortable opening up and expressing your true self.
Pisces	*Neptune*	You are a gentle, imaginative soul who likes to daydream and fantasize. You can use your imagination and creativity to create whole new worlds. You can get lost in your mind, so make sure to ground yourself in the present moment.

The Descendant

The descendant sits between your sixth and seventh houses. The sign here indicates how you relate to and connect with others. It also indicates one of the signs that you may be most compatible with.

The Midheaven

The midheaven sits between your ninth and tenth houses. The sign here indicates how you approach your career and passions and how you go after fulfilling your purpose. The sign that rules over your midheaven is also the energy or quality that can connect you with your higher self or to the power of your soul.

The Nadir

The nadir is located on the cusp between the third and the fourth houses. It indicates your inner needs and unconscious behaviors that you need to become aware of to understand who you are on the deepest of levels. The nadir is a highly spiritually charged point on the chart that indicates the energy or quality you need to tap into to become more authentic. The zodiac ruler of the nadir can give you clues on how to be true to yourself. Read the description of the zodiac sign of your nadir and see if you can be open to this energy.

ASPECTS

Aspects are the way in which the planets in your chart connect with each other. You may notice the aspects as lines crisscrossing in the center of your chart. When certain planets align with each other, they can take on extra significance and carry a more pronounced energy.

THE MAJOR ASPECTS

Aspect	Symbol	Degrees	Indicates
Conjunction	☌	0	Their energy merging as one and becoming stronger
Square	□	90	Tension, but this tension also helps create action
Opposition	☍	180	Balance that needs to be found between the two planets
Trine	△	120	Harmony, protection, and luck
Sextile	⚹	60	Ease, simplicity, harmony

As understanding aspects is advanced, we will not be exploring them further in this book. If you feel ready, make a list of all the squares, trines, sextiles, and so on in your chart and use the planetary descriptions that follow to see how they may interact with one another.

ORBS

Although a square, for example, is classically represented by two planets being 90 degrees apart, a margin of 5 to 10 degrees can be given, depending on the astrologer. Margins such as this are called orbs.

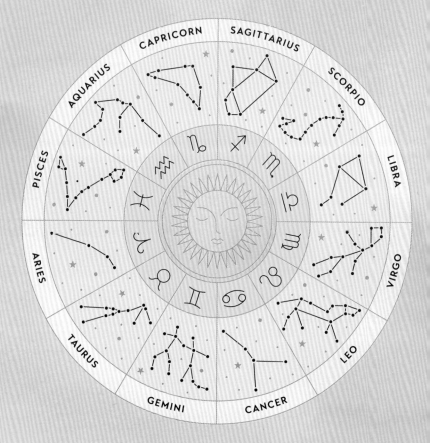

CHAPTER

2

Zodiac Signs

Traditional Western astrology uses twelve zodiac signs, and the essences of these zodiac energies are present in each one of us regardless of what our Sun sign may be. We can tap into these energies through our planets, at the corresponding time of year, or when we are in need of that particular energy in our lives.

ZODIAC SIGNS: ELEMENTS & QUALITIES

The twelve zodiac signs are each assigned an element and a quality. The elements are earth, air, fire, and water. The qualities are cardinal, mutable, and fixed. Think of the qualities like the changing seasons from summer to autumn and winter to spring. The zodiac signs that begin a season are cardinal, the signs at the middle of the season are fixed, and the signs at the end of the season just before they change are mutable.

♈ ARIES   ♉ TAURUS   ♊ GEMINI

♋ CANCER   ♌ LEO   ♍ VIRGO

♎ LIBRA   ♏ SCORPIO   ♐ SAGITTARIUS

♑ CAPRICORN   ♒ AQUARIUS   ♓ PISCES

Elements

- Earth: grounded, stable, solid
- Air: inspired, thoughtful, imaginative
- Fire: passionate, impulsive, energetic
- Water: sensitive, emotional, fluid

Qualities

- Cardinal Signs: leader, starter, headstrong
- Fixed Signs: stubborn, focused, persistent
- Mutable Signs: adaptable, accommodating, flexible

THE MAJOR ASPECTS

Zodiac	Element	Quality
Aries	Fire	Cardinal
Taurus	Earth	Fixed
Gemini	Air	Mutable
Cancer	Water	Cardinal
Leo	Fire	Fixed
Virgo	Earth	Mutable
Libra	Air	Cardinal
Scorpio	Water	Fixed
Sagittarius	Fire	Mutable
Capricorn	Earth	Cardinal
Aquarius	Air	Fixed
Pisces	Water	Mutable

ENERGETIC EXPRESSIONS

Let's now look at the energetic expression of each zodiac sign.

Aries

DATES March 21–April 19

SYMBOL Ram

ELEMENT Fire

QUALITY Cardinal

RULING PLANET Mars

BODY PARTS head, face, eyes

MANTRA I am Energy

KEYWORDS leader, starter, creative, aggressive, innovative

Aries is the first sign of the zodiac. Its energy is synonymous with new beginnings and leadership. Aries is full of life, fiery and expressive, and ready to lead the way. Aries is independent, passionate, impatient, impulsive, and at times, aggressive. We can tune in to Aries energy whenever we are looking to manifest, create, or gain some confidence in getting a project off the ground. Aries energy is naturally invigorating and energizing.

Taurus

DATES April 19–May 20

SYMBOL Bull

ELEMENT Earth

QUALITY Fixed

RULING PLANET Venus

BODY PARTS throat, neck, ears, vocal cords

MANTRA I am Abundant

KEYWORDS reliable, consistent, abundant,
pleasure-seeking, sluggish

Taurus is the second sign of the zodiac. Its energetic quality is like nature in full bloom. It's abundant, sensual, and associated with desire and pleasure. Its energy is slow moving, but it has power to go the distance. It likes to build step by step in a structured and orderly way. Taurus can be sluggish when it comes to change.

It is represented by the bull because of its strength but also stubbornness and sometimes rigid behavior. We can call on Taurus energy when we need to feel grounded, to welcome abundance and a greater sense of self-worth into our lives, and to summon the stamina to go the distance.

Gemini

DATES May 21–June 20

SYMBOL Twins

ELEMENT Air

QUALITY Mutable

RULING PLANET Mercury

BODY PARTS arms, hands, lungs, nervous system

MANTRA I am Expressive

KEYWORDS intellectual, quick-witted, communicator, messenger

Gemini is the third sign of the zodiac. Its essence is about mind, body, and spirit coming together as one. When we are in this state of alignment, we can be ourselves and express whatever is on our mind and in our heart. Gemini is intellectual, social, and adaptable to its environment. We can call on Gemini energy whenever we need confidence and charisma in social settings or when we are looking to communicate our thoughts and feelings.

Cancer

DATES June 21–July 21

SYMBOL Crab

ELEMENT Water

QUALITY Cardinal

RULING PLANET Moon

BODY PARTS chest, breasts, stomach

MANTRA I am Love

KEYWORDS sensitive, intuitive, nurturing, compassionate, moody

Cancer is the fourth sign of the zodiac. It encourages us to open our hearts, to love ourselves, and to work on feeling at peace within ourselves. Cancer can highlight our emotional state, but it also encourages us to accept ourselves, forgive, and move through the world with compassion. We can tune in to Cancer energy whenever we need compassion and nourishment, but also when we are looking for strength to stand up for those we love and for what we believe in.

Leo

DATES July 22–August 22

SYMBOL Lion

ELEMENT Fire

QUALITY Fixed

RULING PLANET Sun

BODY PARTS heart, spine, gallbladder

MANTRA I am Strong

KEYWORDS fiery, bold, fun-loving, playful, creative, proud

Leo is the fifth sign of the zodiac. It is a highly creative, confident, and fun-loving energy. The essence of Leo is light, and its energy guides us to stand tall and shine our light for the whole world to see. Leo has energy we can call on whenever we need a boost of confidence to feel strong and secure in ourselves and when we want to share our creative gifts and talents with the world. Leo is generous: it moves quickly and activates feelings of strength and pride but also fun and laughter. It is highly magnetic and allows us to draw and manifest things into our reality with ease.

Virgo

DATES August 23–September 22

SYMBOL Virgin

ELEMENT Earth

QUALITY Mutable

RULING PLANET Mercury

BODY PARTS digestive system, intestines, pancreas

MANTRA I am Whole

KEYWORDS perfectionist, independent, healing, self-sufficient

Virgo is the sixth sign of the zodiac. It is analytical, practical, and precise. We can call on Virgo energy when we need support with analytical thinking or when we need to get organized. It's also a strong energy to call on for healing. Virgo allows us to remember the inner strength and intuition that we possess and can use to guide us through all sorts of challenges, particularly around our health and well-being.

Libra

DATES September 23–October 22

SYMBOL Scales

ELEMENT Air

QUALITY Cardinal

RULING PLANET Venus

BODY PARTS kidneys, appendix, skin

MANTRA I am Balanced

KEYWORDS relationships, peace, balance, fairness, harmony

Libra is the seventh sign of the zodiac. It allows us to see both sides of the coin and to weigh our options. As the sign of justice, it allows us to fight for what we believe in. Libra guides us to step out of our own inner world and put ourselves in the shoes of others, which lets us develop more thoughtful and fulfilling relationships. We can call on Libra energy to help us through disagreements, to see the other person's perspective, and when we need support to balance our emotions or to give and receive energy in our lives.

Scorpio

DATES October 23–November 21

SYMBOL Scorpion

ELEMENT Water

QUALITY Fixed

RULING PLANET Pluto

BODY PARTS sex organs, reproductive system, colon, bladder

MANTRA I am Transforming

KEYWORDS rebirth, renewal, intense, intuitive, obsessive

Scorpio is the eighth sign of the zodiac. It is highly transformative and guides us to keep digging deeper to turn our wounds into light. When Scorpio energy is free to go with the flow, transformation can happen easily and effortlessly; when the energy is resisted, tension and intensity can be created. Whenever you are going through a significant period of change, call on Scorpio energy to help you navigate through it and remind yourself that endings always lead to new beginnings.

Sagittarius

DATES November 22–December 20

SYMBOL Arrow of the Archer

ELEMENT Fire

QUALITY Mutable

RULING PLANET Jupiter

BODY PARTS hips, sciatic nerve, liver

MANTRA I am Wisdom

KEYWORDS expansive, optimistic, adventurous, scattered, visionary

The essence of Sagittarius, the ninth sign of the zodiac, is freedom. Sagittarius is an optimistic, adventurous, and bountiful energy that we can call on when we are looking for more freedom, play, and excitement in our lives. It is also deeply philosophical and allows us to tap into our inner wisdom. Sagittarius reminds us that we always know the way forward and that we have all we need inside of us; we just have to give ourselves the right guidance and nurturing to release our pearls of wisdom.

Capricorn

DATES December 21–January 19

SYMBOL Sea Goat

ELEMENT Earth

QUALITY Cardinal

RULING PLANET Saturn

BODY PARTS knees, skeletal system, teeth

MANTRA I am Responsible

KEYWORDS ambitious, disciplined, practical, deep, masterful

Capricorn is the tenth sign of the zodiac. It is highly disciplined and wise. We can call on Capricorn energy when we are looking to find more ambition and when we need more motivation to get through life's challenges. Capricorn is earthy, practical, and grounded, but its watery quality allows it to be intuitive too. Capricorn allows us to become masters of whatever challenges we are facing.

Aquarius

DATES January 20–February 18

SYMBOL Water Bearer

ELEMENT Air

QUALITY Fixed

RULING PLANET Uranus

BODY PARTS circulatory system, veins, ankles, calves

MANTRA I am Connected

KEYWORDS humanitarian, progressive, original, rebellious, detached

Aquarius energy is healing. It guides us to remember that we are all connected and that when we work together, anything is possible. Its focus is on what is best for the greater good, rather than the individual. Its energy can create revolutions or inspire new ways of looking at things. We can call on Aquarius energy when we are looking for community, when we want to see things differently, and when we need to shift to higher consciousness.

Pisces

DATES February 19–March 20

SYMBOL Two Fish Swimming in Opposite Directions

ELEMENT Water

QUALITY Mutable

RULING PLANET Neptune

BODY PARTS feet, lymphatic system, immune system

MANTRA I am Intuitive

KEYWORDS receptive, musical, sensitive, timid, spiritual

As the last sign of the zodiac, Pisces is about completion and bringing an end to a chapter of our life journey. Whenever something comes to an end in our life, we can call on Pisces energy to guide us and to remind us that all endings eventually pave the way to new beginnings. Pisces is spiritual and helps us reconnect with the source that we all came from and will all return to. It reminds us that we are never alone on this journey and that we are here as part of a larger unfolding.

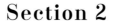

Section 2

· · · · · ● · · · ·

THE BLUEPRINT OF YOUR SOUL

Your Sun sign, Moon sign, rising sign, and lunar nodes paint a clear picture of some of the messages, lessons, and adventures that your soul set out to accomplish in this lifetime. This section explores your Sun, Moon, and lunar nodes and how you can use these energies. Read for both the sign and the house, and then blend the interpretations.

CHAPTER

3

The Sun

ZODIAC RULER Leo

KEYWORDS inner light, core self, ego

RULES OVER leadership, power, energy,
royalty, physicality, vitality

Your Sun sign represents what fuels you, what brings you vitality, and where you feel aligned. By acknowledging the energy behind your Sun sign, you can connect to your purpose and understand what you need to move through this world in a way that honors who you truly are.

THE MEANING OF YOUR SUN SIGN

The Sun represents our life force energy and the core of who we are. It is the foundation of our personality and the key to feeling comfortable and at peace within ourselves. From our center we find our strength, we find our peace, and we find the motivation to fulfill our destiny.

The astrological symbol for the Sun is a circle with a dot in the center. The outer circle represents the world around us, but that dot in the center is the true and constant us. It is our nature, our essence, the core or foundation of our being that is never wavering.

☉♈
SUN IN ARIES OR FIRST HOUSE

RULING PLANET Mars

KEYWORDS independent, entrepreneurial, energetic, leader

MOTIVATION to develop a strong sense of self

CHALLENGES temper, self-centered, impatient

MANTRA I connect with my authentic self

No matter what hardships come your way, when you tune in to that inner Aries fire, you will find the strength, willpower, and determination to make it through to the other side. You shine when you are able to be independent. You like to be in control, and while there may be times when this is necessary, you have to be mindful of becoming overly controlling.

Learning to collaborate with others and release control is a valuable lesson when your Sun is in Aries. You are a strong leader and have an entrepreneurial spirit. You are gifted at coming up with new ideas, but may struggle to find the patience to see them through. This is where learning to collaborate and reach out for support can help you go that extra mile.

THE ASTROLOGICAL NEW YEAR

The Sun entering Aries brings the start of the astrological year and the equinox. This is a time for new beginnings and to honor the cycle of death and rebirth. In the Northern Hemisphere, we can see new life in bloom. In the Southern Hemisphere, the leaves are falling as Mother Nature prepares to rest and retreat.

When not in balance, you can be quick to anger or may find yourself feeling fired up. Learning to process your emotions in a healthy way—and working from spirit rather than ego—will support you staying in alignment. You have a lot of headstrong energy that gives you this wonderful can-do attitude, but learning to shift energy from your mind to your heart will strengthen your intuition and allow you to feel more guided as you move through your journey.

⊙ ♉
SUN IN TAURUS OR SECOND HOUSE

RULING PLANET Venus

KEYWORDS reliable, grounded, patient, creative

MOTIVATION to find true self-worth

CHALLENGES slow, stubborn, overindulgent

MANTRA I am worthy just the way I am

You are grounded, methodical, and practical. This grounded energy comes from your desire to feel secure and stable as you move through your life journey. Deep in your subconscious, feeling safe is a driving motivation. There is nothing wrong with seeking comfort and safety, but you may find yourself stuck if you don't take the leap of faith and make changes as and when they are needed. You love things to be constant and crave routine—but learning to embrace change and go with the flow is a valuable lesson to keep in mind.

True safety is cultivated from within, so be mindful of looking to external sources to fulfill that desire in your life. Part of your journey in this life is learning to feel grounded in your inner power but be adaptable enough to surrender to the flow. Surrendering is not being passive: it's making choices and decisions from a place of trust and listening to the divine intelligence that flows freely within you.

You have the stamina and the patience to move through challenging projects and life events, and it is these qualities that become the mark of your success. When others give up or find the climb too difficult, you are there, still soldiering forward, using your slow and steady approach to win the race.

Lessons of self-worth are important for you. It can be tempting to measure your self-worth in the number of accolades you have or in how much money you make, but know that these measures are never going to fulfill you. When you can say "I am worthy" without any exceptions, you will feel more aligned and connected to your true essence.

You are a master builder and are here to take the seeds that have been planted and nurture them until they turn into forests. As the sign of Taurus is also connected to Mother Earth, you may feel soothed when surrounded by nature.

☉♊
SUN IN GEMINI
OR THIRD HOUSE

RULING PLANET Mercury

KEYWORDS versatile, communicative, social, curious

MOTIVATION to share wisdom and knowledge

CHALLENGES two-faced, manipulative, superficial

MANTRA I attract positive thoughts into my life

You are a keen observer and are always interested in what others are thinking and feeling. Your mind is like a sponge, absorbing information from the world. You are quick-witted, and perhaps you always know the right things to say. Because your mind is like a computer picking up information, it is important that you learn how to filter what comes through. When you don't have a filter, your mind can become overwhelmed and you become prone to overthinking, anxiety, or stress. Having an outlet such as journaling or talking things through can also help.

You are a storyteller and can easily put yourself in another's shoes to convey emotion and help carry through a point. This incredible ability can be tempting to use to manipulate others to get your way, so be mindful of when you find yourself doing this.

As a Gemini Sun, your lesson in this life is to learn how to relax your mind and shift energy into your body. You can be so good at talking and taking in information that you can sometimes forget to actually experience life firsthand. It's one thing to read or think about life, but it's another thing to *live* it, and that's something to keep in mind.

Don't be afraid to live life wholeheartedly. Don't be afraid to step out of the clutches of your mind and get into your body. Take a moment to feel the aliveness of your body right now. When you align that aliveness with your sharp mind, that is when you can really thrive. You are a storyteller at heart, but the most powerful story you can tell is the one that you have walked yourself.

☉ ♋
SUN IN CANCER
OR FOURTH HOUSE

RULING PLANET Moon

KEYWORDS nurturing, emotional, intuitive, protective

MOTIVATION to find a sense of belonging

CHALLENGES defensive, possessive, needy

MANTRA I feel safe within my body, mind, and heart

You have a soft, nurturing, and intuitive nature. Like the Sun rises and sets, you go through your own moods. Sometimes you may feel ready to share your gifts and messages with the world, and other times you need to retreat into your shell and spend time

JUNE SOLSTICE

· · · · · · · · ·

As the Sun enters Cancer, we experience the summer solstice in the Northern Hemisphere and the winter solstice in the Southern Hemisphere. The summer solstice brings the longest day of the year and the full power of the Sun. The winter solstice brings the shortest day of the year and is considered the rebirth of the Sun. The solstice is when the veil between dimensions is thin and we can access the healing power of nature with ease.

in reflection. Your feelings, although overwhelming at times, can become a powerful compass of guidance as you walk your life path. Trusting your intuition and learning to treat your feelings as messengers will help you feel more empowered and connected to your intuition.

Along with intuition, another gift is your ability to nurture and soothe, and to lead with compassion. While this is beautiful, it is important that you also learn how to set healthy boundaries. You are a giver at heart, but when you don't have boundaries, you can quickly become depleted or find yourself feeling taken advantage of.

You are forgiving and supportive, but you need to ensure that the people in your life are respectful and are there for you as you are for them. When you don't feel loved and supported by others, you can feel lonely or feel the need to hide. If you observe this at any point, know the medicine you need is self-love. It is through this that you will find your confidence and strength to protect yourself and your well-being.

Self-acceptance and feeling at home in yourself, no matter what is happening around you, is also an important lesson. When you recognize that home is always a place within you, that is when you can feel the safety and assuredness you need to go into the world and spread your light. Take a moment to ask yourself, "Do I feel at home within myself?" Close your eyes and place your hand over your heart as you ask yourself this question. Listen to the answer that rises up. Sink deeper into this feeling and see if you can find ways to introduce this idea of feeling at home within yourself.

☉♌
SUN IN LEO
OR FIFTH HOUSE

RULING PLANET Sun

KEYWORDS confident, optimistic, creative, loyal

MOTIVATION to share your creative visions

CHALLENGES prideful, attention-seeking, sensitive to criticism

MANTRA I am worthy of love

The Sun feels most at home in the sign of Leo and is able to shine and radiate at its fullest expression. This means you get to experience the true essence of our Sun, the center of our solar system, right within your own center. Having the Sun in Leo makes you magnetic. You have a sunny smile that can light up a room, and your energy is likely to be bold and memorable to those whom you encounter.

You shine brightly and may often find yourself in positions of power or leadership. One of your gifts is learning to stay positive and optimistic when you are facing struggles. You are generous, fun-loving, and may enjoy surrounding yourself with luxury.

When affection and praise are not there, you can easily feel rejected and may find yourself struggling with feelings of inse-curity or needing to behave in a certain way to win the praise and affection that you crave. It is important to become aware of when you are walking this path and to remember that at the end of the day, all that matters is how you feel about yourself. Look-ing for external praise and reward can eventually lead you away from your true self and push you off course. Instead, aligning with your values and working toward what is important is going to lead to a far more satisfying life. Everyone will have an opinion, but the only opinion that matters is your own.

Having the Sun in Leo also indicates that your soul came for a journey of simplicity. You may find yourself wanting to seek the fanfare, but when you connect with your true values, you will find that they are far more simple and far more meaningful. Take a moment now to think about what you value most in life and see if your recent life decisions are aligned with those values. When you focus on your own desires rather than worrying about how they may look in the eyes of others, that is when you can align with your purpose.

You are as radiant as the Sun, and you need not seek approval from others in order to live your best life. Align with the bright, bold Sun that you are and shine your light ahead. It will illuminate the best path for you and guide you on the journey of your soul.

☉ ♍
SUN IN VIRGO
OR SIXTH HOUSE

RULING PLANET Mercury

KEYWORDS independent, efficient, of service, refined

MOTIVATION self-discovery through being of service

CHALLENGES perfectionist, worrier, picky

MANTRA I am perfect just the way I am

You have a sharp mind and strive for perfection in everything you do. You have a serious eye for detail, allowing you to notice things that most people would overlook. This ability is your marker for success; however, you do have to be mindful of chasing perfectionism. Perfectionism is a mask for insecurity and fear. You can use perfectionism to stop yourself from truly being seen and from judgment. Often, this judgment is self-inflicted.

While it is great to strive to do your best, you need to check in and see where this striving comes from. Does it come from a place of fear? Know that your self-worth is not measured in what you achieve or how "perfect" your life seems on the outside. Being authentic and true to yourself is far more rewarding than striving for this perfect image. Learning to accept criticism, and understanding that judgments from others are actually their own insecurities on display can help you stay connected with your center and independence.

Having the Sun in Virgo also gives you innate healing gifts. You may find yourself drawn to the healing arts, or you may be the one your friends call when they need advice. You have a strong intuition and your grounded, earthy energy allows you to access the wisdom of higher realms with ease. This is what ignites your healing qualities, so be sure to embrace this side of your personality and you will find a new way to thrive.

☉ ♎
SUN IN LIBRA
OR SEVENTH HOUSE

RULING PLANET Venus

KEYWORDS fair, peaceful, artistic, negotiator

MOTIVATION to see the self in others

CHALLENGES indecisive, codependent, vain

MANTRA I balance my mind, body, and soul

Part of your soul mission is learning how to create balance in all areas of your life. This balance, however, is one that is born through ease. When you find yourself forcing things or pushing too hard, the scales are not going to be steady and will sway back and forth. Finding balance is about settling into the rhythm of your life no matter where it takes you.

You are a natural mediator. You are compassionate to the struggles of others, and you often feel called to stand up for the injustices of the world. You are a peacekeeper but at times in your life, you may have to ask yourself whether the peace you are fighting for is compromising your own inner peace.

Returning your attention back to yourself is an important reminder when the Sun is in Libra. Part of your destiny is to discover new insights about yourself through the people you meet, but it's also important that you don't lose sight of yourself along the way. The people you encounter and the injustices that you feel passionate about are a mirror drawing you to go deeper so you can uncover your own blocks and the gifts that you can offer the world.

When your energy is scattered, you can find it challenging to make decisions and easy to fixate on the problems of others as if they were your own. When this happens, gently come back to yourself and remember that your true power comes when you feel aligned and whole within yourself and not when you are consumed with what other people are doing. Learning to relate and connect with others is part of your journey, and you may see this manifest in different ways throughout your life. Remember to keep finding balance between the self and others.

☉ ♏
SUN IN SCORPIO
OR EIGHTH HOUSE

RULING PLANET Pluto

KEYWORDS passionate, regenerative, spiritual

MOTIVATION to regenerate through life's experiences

CHALLENGES intense, brooding, suspicious, obsessive

MANTRA It is safe for me to become who I really am

You pick up on the subtle frequencies in your environment and are tuned in to the thoughts and feelings of others. This highly sensitive nature can be challenging, but many gifts can come from it when you learn to master it. Protect your energy through practices such as meditation and working with crystals. You may need to carve out time alone to sit with your thoughts and feelings.

Having the Sun in Scorpio indicates you are here on a journey of transformation. Your struggles and triumphs in this life become important tools of healing for yourself and those around you. You may find that you have a difficult time fitting in or feeling like you belong, but be true to yourself.

As a strong and independent soul, you are not afraid to dive deep into your emotions. You have a gift for facing what is difficult and uncomfortable, and it's important for you to practice. When you are unable to face the sometimes harsh truths around you, you can become obsessive or fixated. This can limit your awareness and the truth of your situation.

Part of your purpose is to keep transforming and shifting through the experiences that life sends your way. The only way to do this is by acknowledging the sometimes painful realities that greet us. By facing the truth, you will find that life takes on a deeper and richer meaning.

☉♐
SUN IN SAGITTARIUS
OR NINTH HOUSE

RULING PLANET Jupiter

KEYWORDS adventurous, energetic, playful, visionary

MOTIVATION to find meaning through life

CHALLENGES unreliable, overly optimistic, insincere

MANTRA Infinite possibilities surround me now

You have the gift of being able to set your goals and make your mark. When you put your mind to something, there is nothing you can't achieve and no adventure is too great! You love your freedom and can really thrive when you feel free to do things your way and in your own time. For your own growth and development, it is important to push yourself out of your comfort zone. Do things that challenge you and stretch your mind to new limits.

For you, life is all about opening yourself to new experiences. You have a curious and inquisitive mind. You are always seeking answers to the bigger questions and you have the gift of being able to see things from a higher perspective. When we go through hardships, it is difficult to see what's ahead or to make sense of our current situation. You, however, have the gift of being able to soar from above and see the truth of what is happening from a higher vantage point. This ability is linked to your soul's purpose in this life, so be sure to use it whenever you are feeling stuck or foggy about the road ahead. Viewing life this way allows you to see that the most difficult roads often lead us to the greatest growth and self-discovery. Life is a journey and your job is to experience all the colors it has to offer.

☉♑
SUN IN CAPRICORN
OR TENTH HOUSE

RULING PLANET Saturn

KEYWORDS ambitious, responsible, disciplined, self-sufficient

MOTIVATION to strive for better

CHALLENGES serious, all work no play, stubborn

MANTRA I bring joy to everything I do

You thrive when you have a goal to work toward, but don't forget to make time for play and to allow your creativity to shine through. Getting too fixated on a goal can block you from experiencing all that life has to offer. You would do better setting intentions rather than goals. Intentions are more open-minded and leave space for the Universe to weave its magic. Setting intentions rather than concrete goals can also keep you out of your head and shift you into what your soul desires.

Along with being incredibly hardworking and ambitious, you are wise beyond your years. The symbol for Capricorn is the sea goat, which is a mythical creature that understands the wisdom of the ocean and the mountains. Take a moment to think about what words are conjured up when you think of the ocean and the mountains. These words may provide some clues on what wisdom you need to lean into at this point in your life.

☉ ♒

SUN IN AQUARIUS
OR ELEVENTH HOUSE

RULING PLANET Uranus

KEYWORDS humanitarian, intellectual, group-oriented, healer

MOTIVATION to lift others

CHALLENGES impersonal, aloof

MANTRA It is safe for me to pave my own way

You love uniting people over common causes. You love to be social, but you are cautious about whom you open up to. You are friendly and ready to guide others, but it can be hard for you to feel comfortable receiving that guidance yourself. You have natural healing abilities but you may be drawn to unconventional healing practices. You are independent and like to carve your own path.

Part of your soul journey is shaking up the status quo to help us all shift our perspectives. One of your key gifts is your revolutionary approach. If you find yourself feeling out of alignment, think about where you may be ignoring the calls of your heart. You are here to innovate, so don't hold back and don't be afraid to walk the path that no one else has walked before. You love to help and guide others, but make sure you don't lose sight of yourself in the process. Your compassion is not complete if it is not returned to yourself as well.

☉♓
SUN IN PISCES
OR TWELFTH HOUSE

RULING PLANET Neptune

KEYWORDS dreamy, creative, musical, intuitive

MOTIVATION to advance in consciousness

CHALLENGES victimhood, exaggerating, scatterbrain, noncommittal

MANTRA I am One with the Universe

You are sensitive to the world around you and may find listening to music, creative activities, or spending time in nature to be therapeutic. The symbol for Pisces is two fish swimming in opposite directions; this represents the illusion of duality. When we shift our consciousness to higher frequencies, we see that everything is one and the same, and it is only our judgment that creates duality.

Along with being intuitive, you also hold strong creative gifts. Giving yourself a creative outlet is important and can prevent you from getting lost in your mind. When your mind is full and you don't have a healthy outlet, your feelings tend to be all over the place and you head into a victim mentality. To prevent this, take ownership over your life and find ways to stay grounded. Although you may have big dreams and spiritual visions, your work right now is to be human, and it's important to find balance and to connect with that. You don't want to forget your spiritual connection either, so be sure to aim for balance whenever possible.

THE LAST SIGN OF THE ZODIAC

· · · ● ● ● ● · ·

As Pisces is the last zodiac sign, it signifies a closure and an ending of a cycle. Regardless of our sign, we may feel this in our own lives as we adjust to the energies of the new year.

4

The Moon

ZODIAC RULER Cancer

KEYWORDS sensitive, emotional, intuitive, nurturing

RULES OVER moods, emotions, ocean, relationship with
mother/femininity, intimate feelings

There is something about the Moon shining brightly in the night sky that reminds us that we are part of a much larger Universe. If you want to feel the effects of the heavens above on your life and develop a deeper relationship with cosmic energies, the best place to start is with the Moon.

☽♈︎
MOON IN ARIES
OR FIRST HOUSE

KEYWORDS confident, adventurous, independent, reactive
MOTIVATION to be the leader of your life
CHALLENGES heated emotions, easily frustrated, egocentric
AFFIRMATION There is nothing I can't handle

You have the courage to speak your mind and share your truth. You need a lot of stimulation and you love trying new things. There is a tendency for your emotions to go from zero to ten pretty quickly, so learn to manage them before they become too overwhelming. You have a natural confidence and inner strength that helps fuel your determination and drive. In your heart you know the way and you know what is right for you, your life, and your body, so be sure to trust your inner wisdom. Learning to accept other people's support and listening to their ideas can create balance and open you to new depths of wisdom and understanding.

☽♉︎
MOON IN TAURUS
OR SECOND HOUSE

KEYWORDS dependable, consistent, nurturing, romantic
MOTIVATION to find stability
CHALLENGES releasing control, fixation, letting go
AFFIRMATION I am grounded in who I am

You crave stability and comfort, and you are in touch with your heart. You like things organized. When change throws you off balance, be patient with yourself and bring your awareness to the present moment rather than allowing yourself to get fixated on the past. Holding on to old pains can block your energy flow, and you may find yourself overspending, overeating, or overindulging. When you find yourself going down this path, it means it's time for you to go within and figure out what is hiding beneath the surface. Try journaling using a prompt such as "I am feeling . . . " and see what comes to the surface. Getting in touch with the truth of the heart is often what you crave. Trust the wisdom of your heart and listen to its messages so you will know the way forward.

☽♊
MOON IN GEMINI
OR THIRD HOUSE

KEYWORDS thinker, creative, storyteller, thoughtful

MOTIVATION to express and share

CHALLENGES disconnecting, gossiping, overanalyzing

AFFIRMATION It is safe for me to share how I feel

It is all too easy for you to get into your head when it comes to your emotions, rather than learning to feel your emotions from the heart. Over time, this can create a disconnect between your body and your emotions. To truly process and shift through your emotions, allow them, especially the more challenging ones, to move through your body. Part of your gifts in this life is learning how to inspire others through your own authentic self-expression. Writing poetry and journaling can also be powerful outlets that can help you tune in to your emotions and digest them. When you explore your emotions on a deeper level and grow in self-awareness, you can help unlock your intuition, allowing you to pick up messages from higher realms.

☾♋
MOON IN CANCER
OR FOURTH HOUSE

KEYWORDS soft, nurturing, intuitive, sensitive

MOTIVATION to feel at home within the self

CHALLENGES boundaries, moody, needy

AFFIRMATION I love and accept myself

The Moon can be your compass and a power source of energy, so tune in to its rhythms and see how you can work with it. You are empathic and can pick up emotions from the world around you. While this makes you beautifully sensitive and intuitive, it is important to also have boundaries and to regularly protect your energy from harsh environments or people. Giving and looking after others can make you feel secure, but make sure that you aren't overdoing it to the point of sacrificing yourself. You are worthy, so don't use your compassionate nature as a way to mask your insecurities. You may find yourself feeling moody at times and needing to retreat into your shell to recharge your batteries. Regularly practicing self-love and acceptance is key and can help you to tune in to the powerful healing and nurturing gifts that having the Moon in Cancer can bring.

☾♌
MOON IN LEO
OR FIFTH HOUSE

KEYWORDS easygoing, creative, generous, fun

MOTIVATION to shine for the world to see

CHALLENGES perfectionism, approval-seeking, dramatic

AFFIRMATION I am proud of who I am

You are easygoing and positive when it comes to your emotions. When you do get upset, it can feel overwhelming, and the fiery, dramatic nature of Leo energy can shine through. To feel safe and secure, you need to feel loved, heard, and seen. You sometimes crave recognition and praise, and you want to know that you are making a difference. Practicing self-love and learning how to become your own biggest champion are valuable lessons for you. Honesty and loyalty are extremely important to you, so even though you can be easygoing and generous, make sure you set boundaries when it comes to those you allow close to you. To embrace your vibrant Leo Moon, be sure to make time for creative activities and allow your feelings to direct your work.

☽ ♍
MOON IN VIRGO
OR SIXTH HOUSE

KEYWORDS sensitive, healer, thinker, logical

MOTIVATION to understand

CHALLENGES overthinking, anxiety, perfectionism

AFFIRMATION I relax and lighten my body

You are sensitive to your emotions and the emotions of others, but you have a way of thinking them through to find ease and calm. Those with the Moon in Virgo are often considered healers. You have to be mindful of overthinking or getting too caught up in your head. Replaying things in your mind is never going to serve you. If you find yourself doing this, it is important to give yourself an outlet such as journaling to release and let go of repetitive thoughts. You may also find yourself prone to worrying and anxiety, so try to remember to soften, let go, and focus on what is in your control. Although it's fine to strive for your best, you tend to hide your insecurities behind perfectionism. Focusing on progress rather than perfection is a good way to shift this mindset.

☾ ♎
MOON IN LIBRA
OR SEVENTH HOUSE

KEYWORDS diplomatic, balanced, compassionate

MOTIVATION staying true to yourself

CHALLENGES projecting, indecisive, people pleasing

AFFIRMATION I am connected to all the Universe

You are diplomatic, fair, and can see things from other people's perspective. By bringing focus back to yourself, rather than projecting onto others, you can feel more decisive and connect deeper with your own true center. If you do find yourself taking on another's emotions, try cleansing your aura through meditation or by taking a bath with salts and essential oils. Knowing who you are and learning to collaborate rather than compromise are valuable lessons. You may also feel called to stand up against injustices and for people who don't have a voice. Although you are a fighter for justice, equality, and fairness, make sure you treat yourself with the same principles that you so freely give to others.

☾ ♏
MOON IN SCORPIO
OR EIGHTH HOUSE

KEYWORDS deep, psychic, sensitive, intense

MOTIVATION transforming emotions

CHALLENGES secretive, dark, obsessive

AFFIRMATION I align with my inner power

You have a keen and sharp intuition and are likely to hold natural psychic gifts. You tend to feel comfortable digging through deeper, darker emotions. You have to be mindful of allowing your emotions to become consuming or spiraling into crisis mode. You tend to hide how you feel from others, and people may accuse you of being secretive. Be mindful of guarding yourself so tightly that you find it hard to create genuine connections with others. As you have a strong intuition and are sensitive to your environment, you may benefit from working with crystals or wearing a protective amulet. When you learn to protect your own energy and follow your intuition more, you will be able to access the transformative powers that having your Moon in Scorpio can bring.

☾♐
MOON IN SAGITTARIUS
OR NINTH HOUSE

KEYWORDS open-minded, philosophical, independent

MOTIVATION seeking new meaning

CHALLENGES opinionated, not taking responsibility

AFFIRMATION What I seek is within

You are adventurous, playful, optimistic, and always looking on the bright side. As Sagittarius is a fire sign, having the Moon here can make you bright and energetic, but it can also make you prone to exaggerating versions of the truth or not taking responsibility for your actions. Your emotions can rise up quickly, but they can also pass just as quickly. To feel safe and secure, you need to be free to express your true thoughts and feelings. At times you may be accused of oversharing or offering your opinion when it's not wanted. You can create healthier relationships by balancing your desire for freedom while still taking into account the emotions and feelings of others.

☾♑
MOON IN CAPRICORN
OR TENTH HOUSE

KEYWORDS practical, wise, moral, responsible

MOTIVATION to use emotions as tools of growth

CHALLENGES insensitive, dismissive, ruthless

AFFIRMATION I choose to feel joy

You are good at staying surface level with your emotions; however, there are real gifts to be had if you can push past any fears or resistance and dive deep into the truth of your heart. When you feel safe to navigate your true feelings and sit with the wisdom and knowledge that you gain, you can use it as a powerful compass to help you navigate through your life.

To feel secure, you like to have long-term goals to focus on and strive for. Keeping a vision board or a list of goals in your room can be a soothing and inspiring reminder for you. You crave success and are highly ambitious, just don't forget to enjoy the ride.

☾♒
MOON IN AQUARIUS
OR ELEVENTH HOUSE

KEYWORDS eclectic, humanitarian, healer

MOTIVATION to find the greater good

CHALLENGES dismissive, insensitive, opinionated

AFFIRMATION I practice compassion

You like to pave your own way, and you tend to speak your mind. You have the natural ability to see what is needed for the greater good, which can also leave you prone to ignoring or dismissing the needs of those closest to you. Getting in touch with your emotions will help you unlock your natural healing gifts and connect you to greater compassion. You may also find baths, chanting, or music to be a source of healing for you. You enjoy your own company, and while you are friendly and warm, it's likely only a few people get to know the true you.

☾♓
MOON IN PISCES
OR TWELFTH HOUSE

KEYWORDS intuitive, musical, spiritual, compassionate

MOTIVATION to turn feelings into inspired action

CHALLENGES victimhood, self-absorbed, overly sensitive

AFFIRMATION I believe in myself

You are likely to be in touch with your own emotions and the emotions of the world around you. Learn how to process your emotions in a healthy way so they don't consume you or leave you feeling overwhelmed. You may find spending time in nature, listening to music, or doing creative projects a good way to help you release and let go of any emotional stress you may be carrying. You may be prone to feeling like a victim or becoming self-absorbed. When you are doing this, shift your thinking and find new ways to empower yourself and expand your mindset. When you learn to master your emotions in a healthy way, you can unlock the psychic, intuitive, and creative gifts of your Pisces Moon.

New Moon
Bring fresh energy
into your life

Crescent Moon
Take steps to
manifest your goals

Balsamic Moon
Retreat and reflect

First Quarter Moon
Be open to change

Last Quarter Moon
Release and let go of the past

Waxing Gibbous Moon
Surrender and
trust the process

Disseminating Moon
Give yourself closure

Full Moon
Claim your power
and allow yourself
to shine

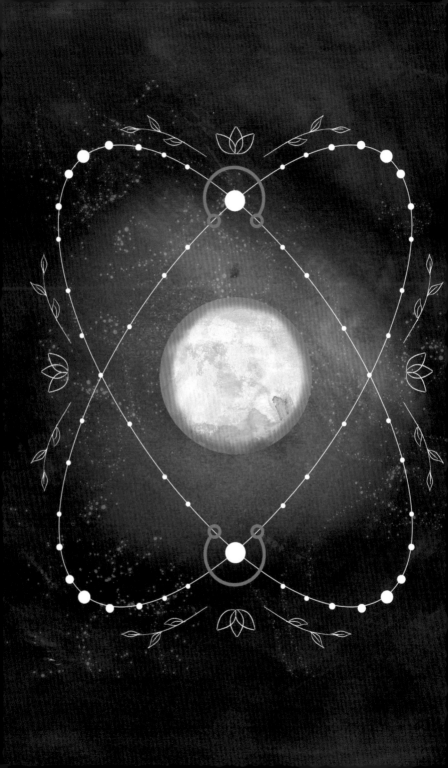

5

Your Lunar Nodes

The lunar nodes are mathematical points calculated between the Sun and the Moon. We have a north and a south node that lie directly opposite each other.

The north node indicates the core lesson of your soul through this lifetime. The path to finding the lessons of your north node begins with your south node. Your north node is where you are heading, and the south node holds the clues for how to get there.

Your south node indicates the lessons that you mastered in your previous incarnations. As you have already mastered these things, if you live or operate from your south node, you could have feelings of stagnancy and a lack of growth. The idea is to embrace your south node talents and skills and use them to pave the way for your north node destiny.

☊♈ NORTH NODE IN ARIES
OR FIRST HOUSE/
☋♎ SOUTH NODE IN LIBRA

In previous lifetimes, you lived a life of service and were always attending to the needs of others. In this life, you need to learn the art of collaboration, rather than compromising how you think and feel. Learn how to be independent rather than letting others make decisions for you. You may fall into people-pleasing tendencies, which can leave you feeling stuck. Real growth comes when you learn it's safe to express yourself. Find your inner warrior, stand firm, and become the leader of your own life.

☊♉ NORTH NODE IN TAURUS
OR SECOND HOUSE/
☋♏ SOUTH NODE IN SCORPIO

In previous lifetimes, you were always helping others to succeed and get ahead. You were a support to those in powerful positions, and it was your keen eye and incredible observation skills that helped them make it to the top. In this life, your purpose is to learn how to build yourself up and to go after your own dreams and wishes. Rather than looking outside of yourself for validation and praise, you need to learn how to create it from within. You need to be your own biggest champion. This life is a journey in establishing your self-worth and confidence—because you are worth it!

☊♊ NORTH NODE IN GEMINI
OR THIRD HOUSE/
☋♐ SOUTH NODE IN SAGITTARIUS

In previous lifetimes, you were a traveler, wanderer, and spiritual seeker. You lived a life of solitude and preferred to go wherever the wind would take you. In this life, you have come to integrate this wisdom into your everyday life. Part of your purpose is also learning how to be social and how to work with others. You have a lot of wisdom to share in this lifetime, so find the confidence to share your incredible knowledge with the world.

☊♋ NORTH NODE IN CANCER
OR FOURTH HOUSE/
☋♑ SOUTH NODE IN CAPRICORN

In previous lifetimes, you were a leader and in charge of organizing and running everything. You had a lot of weight on your shoulders, and many depended on you. In this life, however, you have come to take a more nurturing approach. This doesn't mean you need to ignore the lessons of your previous lifetimes; rather, you need to build upon them by finding a sense of balance. It's okay to ask for help and share the burden with others. You are here to explore all of your emotions and to connect with the voice of your heart.

☊♌ NORTH NODE IN LEO
OR FIFTH HOUSE/
☋♒ SOUTH NODE IN AQUARIUS

In previous lifetimes, you spent a lot of time surrounded by others and focused on the needs and well-being of the group. In this life, learn how to focus on yourself and your own independence: your thoughts matter, your feelings matter, and your concerns are valid. Your skills and abilities from the past make you passionate, empathic, and aware of the world around you. Trust this, and know that when you are in service to yourself, it becomes easier to be in service to others.

Part of your purpose in this life is learning how to follow your creative inspirations and use your imagination to dream up things for your life. Dream big and see where this life can take you.

☊♍ NORTH NODE IN VIRGO
OR SIXTH HOUSE/
☋♓ SOUTH NODE IN PISCES

In previous lifetimes, you didn't like to follow the rules. You lived a creative and imaginative life and were always changing based on your mood. You could get distracted easily and may have found it difficult to find something to focus your attention on. In this life, you need to take this dreamy and creative approach and channel the energy into something focused and grounded. You need to make peace with your mind and learn how to use it as a formidable tool. You are also a natural healer and may be drawn to working in medicine or other healing pursuits.

☊♎ NORTH NODE IN LIBRA
OR SEVENTH HOUSE/
☋♈ SOUTH NODE IN ARIES

In previous lifetimes, you were the warrior and fearless leader. You were in charge of leading the pack and keeping things together. This resulted in you having to wear a mask and never revealing your vulnerability. In this lifetime, you have to take down the mask and learn how to work with others. It's okay to be vulnerable and expose yourself. You also hold gifts of being able to teach and show others how to be their own leader.

☊♏ NORTH NODE IN SCORPIO
OR EIGHTH HOUSE/
☋♉ SOUTH NODE IN TAURUS

In previous lifetimes, you liked to map things out step by step and were routine and methodical about your approach. You were cautious, but it was the right approach. In this life, you need to learn how to take a leap of faith and trust your instincts and intuition a little bit more. Keep pushing yourself, keep challenging your boundaries, and keep motivating yourself to step out of your comfort zone when you find yourself getting caught up in a rigid routine. You don't need to have it all figured out, so keep surprising yourself. Keep your plans in the back of your mind, but allow your intuition and the flow of life to take the lead.

☊♐ NORTH NODE IN SAGITTARIUS
OR NINTH HOUSE/
☋♊ SOUTH NODE IN GEMINI

In previous lifetimes, you loved collecting data and random facts. Knowing gave you a sense of comfort, and you often could be found studying, reading, and learning. Your job in this life is to apply what you have learned in previous incarnations to the real world. Taking action is going to be a big theme of your life. You are also here to learn how to find your own truth. Seek from within.

☊♑ NORTH NODE IN CAPRICORN
OR TENTH HOUSE/
☋♋ SOUTH NODE IN CANCER

In previous lifetimes, you had strong ties to your family, and obligations within the home prevented you from being able to live the life you desired. In this life, you are being given the green light to follow your own goals and dreams. Your lesson is to learn how to cut the cords that are keeping you bound so you can take responsibility for the life you wish to lead. When you find yourself seeking answers or approval from others, check in with yourself and see if you can break this habit by recognizing the strength and determination you have within. Think about what you want, go for it, and don't let others influence the path you take.

☊♒ NORTH NODE IN AQUARIUS
OR ELEVENTH HOUSE/
☋♌ SOUTH NODE IN LEO

In previous lifetimes, you were found in positions of power. You were the center of it all, and many gathered to help support and lift you higher. In this life, you have come to take all of that admiration and attention you received and channel it into being of service to others. As you discover ways to work and collaborate with others, you will also feel far more aligned with your purpose. Your soul has come to help usher us into the "Age of Aquarius," which celebrates this idea that all humans can live in harmony. Your soul is helping pave the way for this, so tune in and allow yourself to be guided.

☊♓ NORTH NODE IN PISCES
OR TWELFTH HOUSE/
☋♍ SOUTH NODE IN VIRGO

In previous lifetimes, when there was a problem to be solved, you focused on finding all the necessary answers and understanding the finest of details. You bring this incredible talent into this life, but you need to learn how to focus on the bigger picture and the hidden meaning within your own soul. Learning to surrender and go with the flow is a far more suitable approach for you in this life. Rather than setting goals and making plans, create an intention and simply trust that the next step will arise in perfect timing.

PLANETS: THE COSMIC MESSENGERS

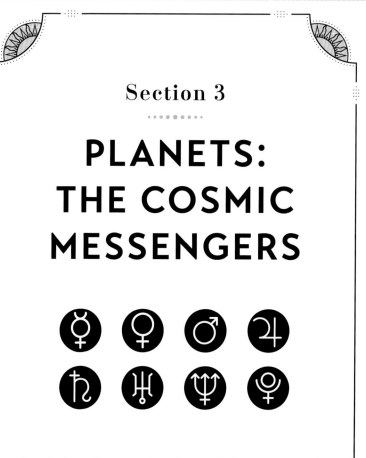

In astrology, there are three types of planets: personal planets, gateway planets, and higher consciousness planets. Each planet holds a particular vibration and emits a frequency that we all have the capacity to feel. The sign and location of the planet at the time of your birth will color how you experience this frequency.

Your Personal Planets

MERCURY   VENUS   MARS

The personal planets make up our base personality: Mercury rules over our mind, Venus rules over our heart, and Mars rules over our ability to take action. As these planets orbit closest to the Sun, their energetic effects are more noticeable, especially on a day-to-day level. The energy of these planets can also influence and trigger us differently, depending on what we are currently going through in our lives.

6

Mercury

ZODIAC RULER Gemini and Virgo

KEYWORDS communication, self-expression, thought processes

RULES OVER technology, cars, travel, moving parts,
phones, journalism/writing, nervous system

Mercury is considered the Messenger of the Gods and governs how we communicate, think, and express ourselves. Mercury can help us unlock the wisdom from our soul and understand ourselves on a mental level. By understanding and connecting with your own Mercury, you can gain deeper insight and awareness into the inner workings of your mind.

In the outside world, Mercury rules technology, transport, and any form of communication. If you need to sign a contract, book a flight, or buy a car, it is helpful to have Mercury in a strong position, because we can think clearly and make the decision that is best for us.

Your personal Mercury sign indicates how you communicate, your state of mind, how you process your thoughts, and where you can receive the best inspiration for your ideas. You can also tune in to the different qualities of Mercury whenever it is touring one of the zodiac signs.

MERCURY RETROGRADE

☿ ℞ From Earth, the planets can sometimes appear to be moving backward. Although this is not actually the case, when a planet does this, it is referred to as being in retrograde. Mercury retrogrades about three or four times a year.

When Mercury goes retrograde, its energy goes inward instead. Our thoughts can become a little foggy and we may find we are met with delays, miscommunications, or technology breakdowns. This is a sign from the Universe that it's time to go within and reflect on the past to see if there were any messages or information we have missed along the way. It is best to pause before moving ahead. It is best to avoid signing long-term contracts or making big commitments when Mercury is in retrograde.

☿♈
MERCURY IN ARIES
OR FIRST HOUSE

INSPIRED BY working out, mental stimulation

COMMUNICATION STYLE direct, to the point, can be harsh

You are a fast thinker and quick on your feet. You seem to know the right thing to say at exactly the right moment, but when you are moving too quickly or not in alignment, you can lash out and say things you may regret. If you are feeling mentally foggy or overwhelmed, vigorous exercise or tackling a challenging task can be a good way to find clarity. You are full of great ideas and may find yourself starting lots of projects. Be mindful of biting off more than you can chew. Your mind can be the birthplace for visionary ideas, so be sure to follow through on the ones that resonate with you the most.

☿♉
MERCURY IN TAURUS
OR SECOND HOUSE

INSPIRED BY rest, contemplation

COMMUNICATION STYLE slow, deliberate, stubborn

You are a methodical, practical thinker, but sometimes you can get stuck in repetitive thought patterns. Learning to trust the flow will help with this, as will breaking down problems into smaller, more manageable steps. You have sharp focus; just make sure you are focused on the things you wish to attract. Your mind works best after plenty of rest. Your mind is always thinking of ways to build, strengthen, and make things better—and this is the gift you can offer to the world.

☿♊
MERCURY IN GEMINI
OR THIRD HOUSE

INSPIRED BY journaling, sharing ideas, reading

COMMUNICATION STYLE conversational, curious, asks lots of questions

Mercury is most at home in the sign of Gemini, so this placement indicates harmony and strong gifts when it comes to communication. You have a sharp mind and strong intellect. You always know the right questions to ask, and you are always going to get to the bottom of things. Your mind can also run in overdrive, turning into a jungle of anxious, repetitive thinking. Getting your thoughts on paper and learning to slow your mind through meditation will help keep it clear and bright. Your mind is the birthplace of storytelling, and this is the gift you can offer to the world.

☿♋
MERCURY IN CANCER
OR FOURTH HOUSE

INSPIRED BY alone time, familiar environments

COMMUNICATION STYLE tender, forgiving, sensitive

Your emotions can get in the way of your thoughts. When this occurs, it is best to take time to pause and deal with your emotions first. You do your best thinking when you are comfortable. You can be a private person, so having a strong support system in which you feel safe to share how you feel is important. Learn to stand up for yourself and not allow your emotions to cloud your judgment. Your mind is the birthplace of nourishment and support. Make sure you are offering this gift to those you love—and to yourself as well.

☿ ♌
MERCURY IN LEO
OR FIFTH HOUSE

INSPIRED BY creative projects, being heard

COMMUNICATION STYLE loud and proud, honest, confident

Mercury is all about the mind, but for you, it is the mind–heart connection that is important. Balancing the heart and mind means acknowledging your feelings, your thoughts, and the voice of your intuition. Turning to creative projects and allowing your thoughts room to breathe can help create stillness and clarity when you are feeling overwhelmed. You also have the natural ability to lead and guide others; stand up for yourself and find your confidence, and your words will flow with ease.

☿ ♍
MERCURY IN VIRGO
OR SIXTH HOUSE

INSPIRED BY mental stimulation, organizing

COMMUNICATION STYLE thoughtful, practical, creative

Mercury is ruled by the sign of Virgo, providing you with a real harmony and flow when it comes to how you communicate; however, you can be prone to perfectionism or worrying about every little thing. Be sure to find balance when this happens. When you claim your own independence, you will be reminded of how capable and worthy you are.

☿♎
MERCURY IN LIBRA
OR SEVENTH HOUSE

INSPIRED BY collaborating with others

COMMUNICATION STYLE fair, rational, indecisive

You like taking a balanced approach when it comes to tackling your mind. Although you like to ponder all that is on offer, sometimes too many options can leave you feeling fatigued. Learning to trust your intuition can help you make quicker and more thoughtful decisions, and it can stop your mind from running in overdrive. Making the "right" decision is making the best choice with what you currently know and feel, and trusting that no matter what comes your way, you are strong enough to make it through.

☿♏
MERCURY IN SCORPIO
OR EIGHTH HOUSE

INSPIRED BY divination, nature, introspection

COMMUNICATION STYLE intense, reserved, poetic

If there is something lurking in the shadows of your subconscious, you have the natural strength and curiosity to venture deeper to bring it into the light. You are not one for small talk, and you need to feel like you are in a safe environment before you can share and express your truth. You have a creative way with words, and you can drop pearls of wisdom that those around you were not expecting. At times you can get wrapped up in the intensity and the seriousness of your thoughts, so make sure you are creating space for lightheartedness and play.

☿♐
MERCURY IN SAGITTARIUS
OR NINTH HOUSE

INSPIRED BY traveling, learning, teaching

COMMUNICATION STYLE outspoken, motivational, direct

You love to look on the bright side of things, and you have a natural gift for motivating yourself and those around you. You love to feel free to express yourself, but sometimes it is better to keep your opinion to yourself unless you have been asked. Giving yourself an outlet such as journaling or a creative project can be a great way to allow thoughts to flow freely and can prevent you from oversharing. You have a mind that is thirsty for knowledge, so make sure you are constantly learning and trying new things.

☿♑
MERCURY IN CAPRICORN
OR TENTH HOUSE

INSPIRED BY researching, fact-checking

COMMUNICATION STYLE practical, blunt, honest

You have a natural ability to see things from a practical point of view, but our past experiences, our judgments, and the way we view the world color our experience of what we see. Part of your journey in this life is learning to clear outdated ways of thinking by remaining open-minded. Integrity and ethics are important to you, and you are always on the quest for a deeper truth. Don't forget to zoom out so you are not missing the bigger picture. When your mind is feeling full and you need a release, researching can be a comfort.

☿ ♒
MERCURY IN AQUARIUS
OR ELEVENTH HOUSE

INSPIRED BY being independent, trial and error

COMMUNICATION STYLE inclusive, technical, soothing

You are a highly innovative freethinker. Don't doubt yourself. Although you have a way of thinking that is out of the box, there is often wisdom to be gained from allowing yourself to explore this. When your mind is full and cluttered, you may find it soothing to think about how you can help others. It is through helping others that you also help yourself.

☿ ♓
MERCURY IN PISCES
OR TWELFTH HOUSE

INSPIRED BY music, retreat

COMMUNICATION STYLE flowery, heartfelt, indirect

Your mind is full of daydreams, and you may find it difficult to keep your thoughts rooted and grounded in your present reality. You have an abstract way of thinking about things. Sometimes, what you are thinking and feeling cannot be expressed in words. Although you may struggle to "think" your way through life, you most definitely have the ability to "feel" your way, and this can become your superpower. Your soul is here to express its abstract, dreamy, and creative thoughts, so allow yourself to wander. Return to the present as often as you can and recognize the value in the here and now.

CHAPTER

7

Venus

ZODIAC RULER Taurus and Libra

KEYWORDS beauty, femininity, love, divine, intuitive

RULES OVER relationships, money/profits, fashion,
beauty industry, creative work

Venus is the planet of love, beauty, romance, creativity, and money. Venus energy is magnetic and is attuned to the vibration of our heart center. Whenever there is a matter involving the heart, we can look to Venus for clues and guidance. Along with being a guiding compass for our heart, the sign Venus was in at the time of our birth can signal what we need to feel emotionally fulfilled, what we are attracted to, and what we value.

♀♈
VENUS IN ARIES
OR FIRST HOUSE

LOVE IS passionate, at first sight, physical

You are fiery and passionate, and you tend to fall in love fast! You can trust the wisdom of your heart, but be mindful not to rush too quickly into things before you are certain.

You know what you want. You have confidence when it comes to putting yourself out there and telling others how you feel. People are drawn to you for your independence and your innovative way of approaching life. Surround yourself with people who respect you and can handle your bright inner flame.

♀♉
VENUS IN TAURUS
OR SECOND HOUSE

LOVE IS trust, respect, richer over time

While Venus is the planet of love and beauty, it is also the planet of money. Venus in Taurus indicates that creating a healthy relationship with money is part of your purpose in this life. Taurus is also associated with self-worth, so this placement can indicate a need to open yourself to receiving the gifts and bounties of the Universe without allowing yourself to get trapped in thoughts of scarcity or that you are not good enough. Focusing on gratitude will help appease this, so whenever you notice the voice of fear or doubt creep in, acknowledge it, but also look to what you feel grateful for.

♀♊
VENUS IN GEMINI
OR THIRD HOUSE

LOVE IS fun, being connected, being heard

This is a fun and flirty placement! Venus in Gemini loves to talk, ask questions, and make the other person the center of attention. Communication is important in all relationships, but for you it can also be the key to your heart. When you feel heard is when you feel the safest to let your guard down. When you are feeling insecure or defensive, your Gemini twin can rear its head and pretend you are unfazed or not bothered. You are a master with words, but you also need to be careful of promising more than you can offer. Make sure your words are aligned with the truth of your heart and you will always feel in balance.

♀♋
VENUS IN CANCER
OR FOURTH HOUSE

LOVE IS giving, compassionate, safe

You are soft, sensitive, and cautious with love. You are heart-driven and tend to feel the emotions of the world. You can trust your intuition and your first impressions when it comes to meeting people. The more confident and secure you feel inside, the easier it will be for you to open up to others. Learning to love yourself is key if you want to be able to learn to love others. While receiving love is important, when Venus is in Cancer, the lesson of self-love is very pronounced.

♀♌
VENUS IN LEO
FIFTH HOUSE

LOVE IS exciting, passionate, intense

You are highly creative and fun-loving. You have a magnetic aura, and you are likely to find that people are drawn to you for your good vibes and your ability to always have a good time. There is no doubt this is a magnetic and attractive placement. Part of your purpose in this life is allowing yourself to shine. Boost your confidence and learn to be comfortable in the spotlight. Share your heart energy and creative wisdom with the world, as it will lead you to success.

♀♍
VENUS IN VIRGO
OR SIXTH HOUSE

LOVE IS independence, healing, intuitive

You are independent, and it is important for you to be connected to the truth and wisdom of your heart at all times. You deserve to channel all your passion and love into your personal projects and what excites and calls to your spirit. On a soul level, you have lots to do in this life, and you would be best suited to a partner who can acknowledge this and support you as you do your work. It's okay to ask for support when you need it.

♀︎♎︎
VENUS IN LIBRA
OR SEVENTH HOUSE

LOVE IS togetherness, peaceful, working as one

How you relate and connect with others is an important soul journey for you in this life. Those around you can be like a mirror, helping you understand your own triggers and your own truth. On a soul and energetic level, we are all connected; we are all One. We are all in this together, and learning to work with others, no matter how different they may be from you, is all part of your journey. Learn to see yourself in others, but also learn to stay true to yourself and your individual spark.

♀︎♏︎
VENUS IN SCORPIO
OR EIGHTH HOUSE

LOVE IS intimate, private, intense

Intimacy and physical touch are important to you in your relationships and are a part of how you build your connections with others. While you are a romantic at heart, you are also a private person, and it is not always easy for you to put yourself out there and open up. Find the confidence to share how you feel or approach whomever you are interested in. When you do feel safe to open your heart, you can feel love intensely. Make sure you are keeping yourself grounded. Part of your purpose in this life is learning to evolve and become more of your true self through the lessons and journeys of your most important relationships.

♀♐
VENUS IN SAGITTARIUS
OR NINTH HOUSE

LOVE IS friendship, growth, inspirational

You may find many are attracted to your laugh, your smile, and your easygoing attitude. You are attracted to people with big ideas who think differently about the world. You are a traveler and an explorer at heart, and you need someone who is going to be willing to take this journey with you. You may find you are drawn to connecting and forging relationships with people who have a different culture than your own. You crave your independence and freedom. Staying focused on your own path and finding a partner who is supportive of this is important for your journey in this life.

♀♑
VENUS IN CAPRICORN
OR TENTH HOUSE

LOVE IS supportive, patient, better with time

You love to be in relationships where you can share your goals and dreams and support each other as you both climb your own mountains. Success is highly appealing to you; just don't forget to keep tuning in and listening to the wisdom of your heart. Don't be afraid to dive deep into your emotions, and don't feel the need to justify or rationalize them away with your thoughts. Connecting deeper with your emotions will help you forge meaningful connections with others.

♀♒
VENUS IN AQUARIUS
OR ELEVENTH HOUSE

LOVE IS freedom, empathy, generous

You have a big heart and are drawn to helping, supporting, and lifting up others. You also crave your freedom and don't want to feel like you are being held back or tied down by anyone. You can feel a little exposed when it comes to opening your heart or being in the spotlight of a conversation. To enter into deeper, more committed partnerships, you need to learn how to let down your guard and allow yourself to receive. Make sure there is an equal balance of give and take in your relationships. When you are feeling heavy in your heart or overwhelmed by your emotions, you may find that helping others can lighten your load.

♀♓
VENUS IN PISCES
OR TWELFTH HOUSE

LOVE IS spiritual, for all, truth

You are highly creative and in tune with the intuitive wisdom of your heart. You are romantic and sensitive, and you are interested in relationships that allow you to connect on the deepest of levels. You feel attracted to another when you can explore the feelings and emotions bubbling beneath the surface. You are sensitive to your emotions and the emotions of others. Make sure you are protecting your energy by setting boundaries and surrounding yourself with people who have your best interests at heart. Part of your purpose in this life is to connect with your creativity, intuition, and spirituality. Merging the three can help activate your passions and open your heart center even wider.

VENUS COMPATIBILITY FOR LOVE AND FRIENDSHIP

Your Venus Sign	Most Compatible Venus Signs
Aries	Aries, Leo, Libra, Scorpio, Sagittarius
Taurus	Taurus, Virgo, Libra, Scorpio, Capricorn
Gemini	Gemini, Virgo, Libra, Sagittarius, Aquarius
Cancer	Cancer, Scorpio, Capricorn, Pisces
Leo	Aries, Leo, Sagittarius, Aquarius
Virgo	Taurus, Gemini, Virgo, Capricorn, Pisces
Libra	Aries, Taurus, Gemini, Libra, Aquarius
Scorpio	Aries, Taurus, Cancer, Scorpio, Pisces
Sagittarius	Aries, Gemini, Sagittarius, Leo
Capricorn	Taurus, Cancer, Virgo, Capricorn
Aquarius	Gemini, Leo, Libra, Aquarius
Pisces	Cancer, Virgo, Scorpio, Pisces

8

Mars

ZODIAC RULER Aries and Scorpio

KEYWORDS taking action, motivation, inner warrior,
impulses, ambition, competition

RULES OVER wars/weapons, energy levels, sex, surgery, accidents

Mars is the warrior planet that exudes a fiery passion. Its energy helps us take action in our lives, and it keeps us motivated and following the path that makes us feel alive and filled with purpose. Where Mars was at the time of your birth can indicate where you most express your energy, where you feel most motivated, your passion, and what drives you in this life. It can also indicate your inner warrior and how you face the battles and struggles that life brings your way.

While you have your natal Mars to work with, you can also tune in to the many messages of Mars as it makes its way through the zodiac.

BORN WITH MARS IN RETROGRADE?

....

♂ ℞ If you are born with Mars in retrograde, you need to make an extra effort to access your Mars qualities. However, this extra effort is only until you find what works for you.

♂♈
MARS IN ARIES
OR FIRST HOUSE

MOTIVATION to create and lead others

Having Mars in Aries gives you a strong motivation and will-power to do things and to act. This is an energetic placement, so make sure you are giving yourself an outlet to express this energy. When you feel depleted or burnt out for prolonged periods, it could be because you are expressing your energy in a way that is not fulfilling to your true self. Your Mars needs the right kind of stimulation. Think about how you can bring more energy into your life, focusing on your passions and the things that light a fire inside of you. You are a born warrior, so make sure you are tapping into that innate strength you were born with.

♂♉
MARS IN TAURUS
OR SECOND HOUSE

MOTIVATION slow and steady wins the race

Taurus likes to move slowly and methodically, whereas Mars wants to move quickly and act! This can create a feeling of restlessness, in which you may feel caught between jumping in to take action and waiting for the right moment. While you want to look before leaping, be mindful of overthinking it or getting so stuck in indecision that it prevents you from moving at all. Finding balance between thinking things over and taking that leap of faith is an important life lesson for you. Your methodical approach sees that eventually you will always get to where you need to be. Taking small, consistent steps can bring great rewards in time.

♂♊
MARS IN GEMINI
OR THIRD HOUSE

MOTIVATION think your way through

You are always asking questions and trying to get to the bottom of things. While this may be favorable at work, you may need to learn to slow down in your personal life and learn to savor the time you share with others. You thrive in busy environments and feel best when you can have your hands in multiple projects at once. Be mindful of spreading yourself too thin. When you become overwhelmed, it can be harder for you to keep your focus and get things done.

♂♋
MARS IN CANCER
OR FOURTH HOUSE

MOTIVATION make love, not war

In Cancer, the warrior is not interested in fighting or pursuing war; instead, it wants to return to what is comfortable and safe. Yet, when it does, it cannot express its fullest qualities. You need to learn how to be independent while also honoring your feelings and need for security. You need to learn how to create a comfortable environment in the home that makes you feel safe and welcomed. You need to have somewhere soft and cozy to land, for when you do, you will feel more confident and comfortable taking risks in the outside world.

♂♌
MARS IN LEO
OR FIFTH HOUSE

MOTIVATION self-belief

The Mars in Leo warrior sets out to battle feeling confident— and extremely well dressed, too! Your confidence is your strong point, so make this work for you. If you align with your authentic self, you can find your confidence and live for yourself rather than for others. Connect with that fire of passion burning inside of you and ride off on your gallant and beautiful horse. Your confidence and willpower bring you all the luck and success you need in this life.

♂♍
MARS IN VIRGO
OR SIXTH HOUSE

MOTIVATION independence

The warrior in Virgo is independent and doesn't need help. It wants to be free and independent to do things its own way. The Mars in Virgo warrior has a precise plan and knows every move it will make down to the second. No one else could understand this level of precision, so it is better to go it alone. While a lot can be achieved in this way and there is success to be had, learning to work with and trust others to help you can be more effective. There is no doubt you have the strength and tenacity to fight any battle single-handedly, but just because you can doesn't mean you should.

♂♎
MARS IN LIBRA
OR SEVENTH HOUSE

MOTIVATION justice for all

The warrior in Libra never wants to choose sides; it wants to talk things over and find a peaceful and fair resolution that will make everyone happy—but this rarely can make everyone happy. Learning when to step back and not involve yourself in other people's problems is also a good skill. While you want to keep the peace, it is your inner peace that is most important. As you move through your life, you may be challenged in this area. But, as you get more comfortable and confident in your own skin and learn to connect with your truth, it will become easier for you to put your inner peace first and foremost.

♂♏
MARS IN SCORPIO
OR EIGHTH HOUSE

MOTIVATION inner knowing

The warrior Mars in Scorpio is thrifty, a little manipulative, and always thinking ten steps ahead. You are clever and cunning and have the mind of a brilliant chess player. You are also a natural detective and can see things many others would miss. You can be a closed book, but when you learn to trust yourself, it's easier to trust those around you. Letting your guard down and allowing yourself to be vulnerable can also grant you access to a new set of skills, ones that are more intuitive and even psychic. Don't close off to the wisdom of your heart. Your heart can help you see things that even the mind can miss.

♂♐
MARS IN SAGITTARIUS
OR NINTH HOUSE

MOTIVATION freedom

While Mars in Sagittarius can sometimes be unreliable, there is a strong urge to go with the flow of life and not miss out on the random and exciting opportunities you encounter along the way. Keeping a certain level of spontaneity in life can relieve feelings of stagnancy. Just be mindful of making promises you can't keep. You need a certain level of freedom, but you also need structure and routine to get things done. Honor your desire to do things your own way and in your own time, but be sure to take responsibility and create boundaries for yourself.

♂♑
MARS IN CAPRICORN
OR TENTH HOUSE

MOTIVATION ambition

The Capricorn Mars warrior knows how to lead and is relentless. Success is a driving motivator for you in this life. When you put your mind to something and want to achieve it, there is nothing you can't do. You are driven and motivated; just make sure you are stopping to enjoy the journey. You can get in the habit of chasing the goal without giving thought to the steps you have to take to actually get there. If you don't enjoy the journey, is the destination still worth it? Only you can be the judge of that.

♂♒
MARS IN AQUARIUS
OR ELEVENTH HOUSE

MOTIVATION helping others

The Mars in Aquarius warrior loves to lead but wants to do so in a way that serves the greater good and not just themselves. Being there for others is part of your calling, but if you are not there for yourself, there is no way you can truly give to others. It is your inner spark that is so valuable and helpful to others, but you can't pour from an empty cup. Work on filling yourself so you overflow, and from that overflow, doing the work and sharing the message of your soul.

♂♓
MARS IN PISCES
OR TWELFTH HOUSE

MOTIVATION ease

The Mars in Pisces warrior has fought many battles, but now it realizes life is not about being at war. Don't be at war with yourself any longer. This energy is about surrendering to the flow of your life and allowing things to be as they are rather than fighting them. It is okay to make mistakes, and it is okay if things aren't perfect. Staying present, staying in your aware-ness, and allowing yourself to be as you are can be a powerful way to instigate positive change and bring ease.

The Gateway Planets

JUPITER   SATURN

The gateway planets are the bridge between the personal planets and the planets of higher consciousness. These gateway planets are Jupiter and Saturn along with the asteroid Chiron. These celestial bodies begin taking us from our outward personality into the deeper depths of our inner personality. By walking the bridge that the gateway planets provide, and working through the lessons and gifts they offer, we can step into a higher state of being and elevate our consciousness to new levels of awareness and enlightenment.

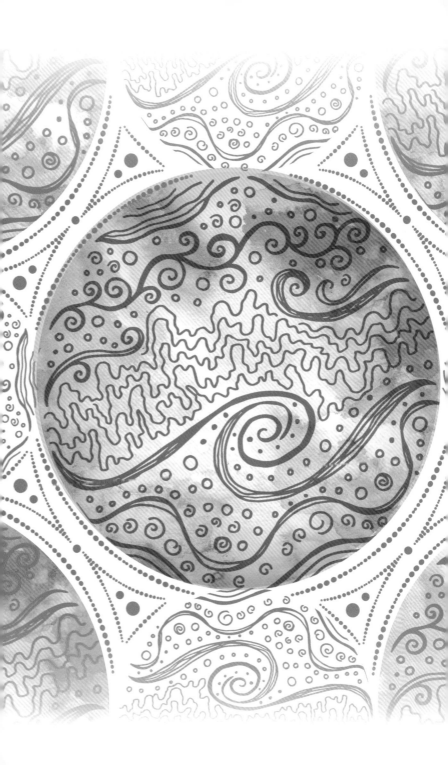

9

Jupiter

ZODIAC RULER Sagittarius

KEYWORDS abundance, expansion, opportunity

RULES OVER fame, fortune, law, higher education,
religion/philosophy, international travel

Jupiter is the largest planet in the solar system and has a
strong magnetic force that can help expand our mind,
our heart, and the opportunities around us. Our Jupiter
can also indicate natural strengths and talents, and where
we are given an extra sprinkling of luck. Jupiter reveals to
us where we can thrive and shows us the areas of our lives
where we may find we have natural gifts and talents.

Let's consider Jupiter through the zodiac. Remember,
you can always tune in to this energy when Jupiter is in a
particular zodiac sign.

....

♃ Ŗ
ᕽ

Being born with Jupiter in retrograde indicates you have the ability to bring luck, abundance, and success to those around you. Through giving to others, you find your own way to success too. Jupiter retrograde can also indicate that part of your soul purpose is to unlock the buried treasures that are nestled within you. You came into this life with a lot of wisdom, and as you dig deeper, you will be able to uncover these nuggets of wisdom to guide you on your journey.

♃♈
JUPITER IN ARIES
OR FIRST HOUSE

GIFT independent self-starter

Jupiter in Aries indicates your soul is here to bring a fresh new start to your life in some way. Part of your journey is learning how to trust your ideas and innovations and take the first steps to bring them into reality. Don't worry about having all the answers; sometimes starting first then seeing where you end up is the approach to take. Your gifts and talents lie in your ability to command respect and lead others.

While you are direct and can see the path clearly ahead, be mindful of closing off your mind to the ideas of others. You have a strong energy and a great enthusiasm for life. You know what you want, so trust yourself and know there are no limits on what you can achieve.

♃♉
JUPITER IN TAURUS
OR SECOND HOUSE

GIFT steady success

While Taurus likes things to remain stable and consistent, Jupiter encourages you to move, keep trying new things, and not stay in one place for too long. In this life, it is all about finding a balance between these two energies.

When was the last time you did something new for the first time? Doing new things can feel scary, especially as we get older. Even though trying something new can feel intimidating at first, make it a point to challenge yourself a few times a year by learning a new skill or trying something new. Keep your safe comfort zone, but give yourself permission to explore and change things up too.

♃♊
JUPITER IN GEMINI
OR THIRD HOUSE

GIFT thoughtful communication

You have a sharp, intelligent mind and this is where your power lies. Keep your mind stimulated with the right kind of input. Monitoring your thoughts and ensuring that they are not self-limiting or self-deprecating is important for you. Creating a beautiful and peaceful mental state is something that is going to serve you well and will allow you to access the gifts and power of your mind. You also have natural skills and talents when it comes to working with your hands. You are good in all areas relating to communication. With a clear mind, you will be able to find the solution to every problem and to every struggle that greets you on this life journey.

♃♋
JUPITER IN CANCER
OR FOURTH HOUSE

GIFT compassionate protector

Although people are drawn to your warmth, part of your journey in this life is learning how to fill your cup with self-love and nourishment. You need to embrace the idea of receiving, and the main thing you need to learn how to receive is your own love, compassion, and forgiveness. Your task is to remove all the blocks and boundaries you have created that keep love out of your own heart. You have a lot of love to give in this life, not just to yourself but to others as well. Everyone deserves to receive love, but be mindful about who you are choosing to allow in your presence. Sometimes loving from a distance is okay.

♃♌
JUPITER IN LEO
OR FIFTH HOUSE

GIFT creative confidence

You are here to share your message with the world, but there are a few speed bumps to watch for along the way. You may crave attention or feel like your journey needs to be extra special compared to others. Be mindful of disregarding the journeys of those around you.

Leading your life from the heart is something you are gifted at doing, but if you have forgotten or are unsure of what it feels like to lead from your heart, take a moment to tune in. Place your hand over your heart and breathe here for a moment, feeling your heart energy. Connect to what your heart is feeling right now and listen to what arises. What you hear is the sound of your heart connecting and communicating with you. Keep practicing this heart communication and eventually it will strengthen with time. Your heart holds the key to your life, so make sure you are connected and listening to its wisdom.

♃ ♍
JUPITER IN VIRGO
OR SIXTH HOUSE

GIFT natural healer

While Jupiter wants to look at the bigger picture, Virgo wants to focus on the details—and this can create a conflict when it's not kept in balance. The next time you find yourself getting caught up in the details, see whether you can allow a little more room for the bigger picture to emerge. And, the next time you are focused on the bigger picture, see whether you can zoom in a little bit so you are not missing any of the important details. You also have the innate and natural gift of being able to rebuild yourself after hardship and trauma. You are a natural healer, and no matter what challenges come your way, you always have the ability to work through them and rise up stronger.

♃ ♎
JUPITER IN LIBRA
OR SEVENTH HOUSE

GIFT understanding others

As Jupiter reveals more of the picture, Libra is looking to see how it can fit what it sees under the label of good or bad. As more information is revealed, however, we change our awareness of what is good and what is bad. While we cannot put things into compartments, we can trust and see that balance is always achieved. It is a law of nature. When something ends, something else is born. When a door closes, another opens. This is nature and the laws of the Universe in action. Part of your purpose is learning how to find more wholeness. It is about learning to stop judging or getting caught up in what's good or bad and just allowing yourself to stay present with whatever life brings your way without feeling the need to label it. When you learn to bring more acceptance to your life and move out of judgment, you will unlock more of your blessings and gifts that this life has to offer you.

♃ ♏
JUPITER IN SCORPIO
OR EIGHTH HOUSE

GIFT strong intuition

It is part of your purpose in this life to keep shining a light on your shadows so you can shift and move past them. While you may try to bury your pains, traumas, and truthful feelings, they will never stay hidden for long. Jupiter is always there, ready to shine its light and expose them so they can be transformed once and for all. All through your life you may feel you are on this journey of peeling back the layers you have surrounded yourself in, to find a deeper truth. You were blessed with the powers of transformation. You know how to take the darkness and shine your light on it. You know how to honor what the darkness is trying to show you, but you also have the awareness that the darkness is no place to stay.

♃♐
JUPITER IN SAGITTARIUS
OR NINTH HOUSE

GIFT positive mind-set

With Jupiter in Sagittarius, you are motivated to achieve your goals. You are always looking for ways to open your mind and heart to life and the experiences it brings your way. As you fill your life with rich and rewarding experiences, you keep sinking deeper into who you are and what fills you up in this life. Part of your journey is learning how to return to joy, and you can achieve that by quenching your curiosity for life and all it has to offer. Don't be afraid to keep searching and exploring new experiences. Just keep in mind that it is also important to stay grounded and keep a sense of routine and structure. You are a free soul, and that is beautiful, but you also need to learn how to be an active participant in this earthly reality.

♃♑
JUPITER IN CAPRICORN
OR TENTH HOUSE

GIFT dedicated ambition

Jupiter in Capricorn is highly ambitious and will never back down. You are extremely motivated and will make it your life's mission to figure out how to turn your dreams into tangible realities. Building a legacy is important to you, but remember this: Your legacy is not in how many goals you achieve; it is in how you treat others and how you show up for the ones you love. Your legacy is built in the small actions you take every single day.

Success and ambition are all huge motivators and drivers for you in this life. Just keep in mind that this journey can have a price to pay if you lose sight of everything and everyone else in the process.

♃ ♒

JUPITER IN AQUARIUS
OR ELEVENTH HOUSE

GIFT seeing the bigger picture

You are a humanitarian at heart and are always thinking of ways to make this world a better and safer place. It is through your generosity and your expansive vision for the world that you are able to also grow in richness for yourself. You have big dreams and you are going to need support to bring them to light. Using your generous heart to give and help others can bring great luck and fortune. The community and connections you build in this life are like family to you and, in turn, they are all like family to each other. You make life richer and more rewarding for those around you. Life is made for sharing, and you are leading the way.

♃ ♓
JUPITER IN PISCES
OR TWELFTH HOUSE

GIFT paving your own way

Life has so much to offer you, and you are here to taste a little bit of it all. Don't feel like you have to choose just one path in this life. Even though our soul comes into this life with a certain "programming" and a destiny to move through, it would defeat the purpose if we were given access to the ins and outs of what this may be. Learning to embrace this as the plan of your life can actually give you more direction and can help you feel grounded as you move through your life. Your lessons and gifts in this life are learning to surrender, go with the flow, and trust that your skills are always sharpening when you reach the roughest seas.

10

Saturn

ZODIAC RULER Capricorn

KEYWORDS discipline, responsibility, authority, dedication

RULES OVER relationship with father/masculine, maturity, big business, government, authority figures, laws, rules, boundaries

Saturn is like a strict teacher and is one of the most profound gateway planets on the journey to deeper truth, knowledge, and awareness. Saturn can bring hard lessons, but it is through those lessons that we can grow and achieve the most self-discovery. Just like that strict teacher, whenever we hand in our homework on time and excel in our tests, we get rewarded—the only difference is that these tests and lessons can't be learned through a textbook!

♄℞ Saturn spends at least six months of the year in retrograde. Being born with Saturn in retrograde indicates that most of your growth in this life is on an internal level, rather than on an external one.

♄♈
SATURN IN ARIES
OR FIRST HOUSE

KARMIC LESSON expanding and deepening how you define yourself

You are a pioneer, and part of your purpose in this life is to create something new and bring bold new innovations to the planet. By expressing your unique essence, you are able to shine your light and lift and inspire others. Part of your karma in this life is in learning how to tame your inner fire and stand up for yourself, while also taking into consideration those around you. You may have the tendency to run or want to retreat when things get challenging or uncomfortable. Over the years, learning to stay and navigate through these challenges, rather than run from them, can help you achieve the most growth and reward.

♄♉
SATURN IN TAURUS
OR SECOND HOUSE

KARMIC LESSON knowing your true self-worth and what you value

You are extremely hardworking and tend to view life as a challenge that needs to be overcome. You may feel concerned with safety and create boundaries that give you a sense of stability and routine.

Be mindful of boxing yourself in too much. While you like to take a methodical and measured approach to everything you do, sometimes you also have to trust your heart and believe that things will always work out how and when they are supposed to. Part of your karmic lessons in this life also revolve around where you choose to spend your energy. This includes how you choose to spend your time, whom you choose to spend your time with, and how you choose to spend your money. Getting clear on your values will help with this.

♄♊
SATURN IN GEMINI
OR THIRD HOUSE

KARMIC LESSON speaking your truth and using your voice

Part of your karmic lessons in this life revolve around communication. In this life, your words, or lack of words, can get you into trouble at times. Mindful communication is an extremely difficult skill to master, but it is an important one for you. As you master your ability to communicate, you are going to have to also be mindful to not use your skills to manipulate or con others into getting your own way. When you do, strict teacher Saturn can bring some hard knocks, forcing you to get into line. Your purpose in this life is to take responsibility for the words that you speak and the motives behind them. When your motives are aligned with your true self, you are going to find that they are able to open doors for you and bring exciting opportunities. We all grow from challenges: part of this experience in life is making mistakes, or taking risks that sometimes don't work out. Keep checking in with yourself and ensure that your morals and values are aligned with where you want them to be.

♄♋
SATURN IN CANCER
OR FOURTH HOUSE

KARMIC LESSON creating boundaries even with those you love

Part of your karmic lessons in this life stems from your upbringing and the relationship that you have with your family. Before you came into this body, you existed as an eternal soul in another realm. As this eternal soul, you decided the lessons and journey you wanted to experience in this life, and you chose your family based not on how amazing they would be, but how much they would support your soul journey and the things that you wanted to learn in this life.

Part of your journey is learning to break out of family patterns and cycles that don't align with you and to show that a new and better way can be achieved. Learning to love yourself is a key to finding the strength and the confidence to break the generational cycles that are playing out. Another way to look at this is ending the emotional traumas that are carried through your generational bloodline.

♄♌
SATURN IN LEO
OR FIFTH HOUSE

KARMIC LESSON putting yourself and your ideas out there

Part of your karmic lessons is learning to navigate the abundance that is always around you. Abundance is all around us and comes in many different forms. For you, learning to appreciate the abundance in all things and in all states of your life is what the journey is all about. You may experience challenges with money.

Chasing status, luxury, and riches can sound like a good idea, but it is not going to serve you in this life.

You may feel blinded by the bright lights of riches and fame throughout your life, but know that true happiness and fulfillment is an inside job. It is learning to see the bigger picture and to understand that all jobs are important and all people are important. An important part of your life journey is to find respect for yourself no matter how "successful" you deem yourself to be, and to have respect for others, no matter how successful you deem them to be.

♄♍
SATURN IN VIRGO
OR SIXTH HOUSE

KARMIC LESSON creating healthy habits

You have great discipline and strive for perfection in everything you do. You like to follow the instructions, but sometimes in life, not everything comes with instructions to follow. It is moments like these when you do your most growth work. While growth can be challenging, when you have only your inner wisdom to rely on, that is when you make some of the bravest, boldest, and most successful leaps of your life. When you connect with your soul through practices such as meditation, healing work, and the like, you can step into a new, independent power that can help you take the instructions and work of others and add your own unique flair and spin.

♄♎︎
SATURN IN LIBRA
OR SEVENTH HOUSE

KARMIC LESSON building healthy relationships

Many of your karmic lessons in this life revolve around your relationships and the people you encounter on your journey. You are learning to stand up for yourself and set your boundaries, so you are not losing yourself in the thoughts and feelings of others. But you are also learning how to connect and create deeper and more loving relationships in the process. On a spiritual level, life may also highlight to you how those around you can be a mirror for your own triggers and what is happening within you. Setting boundaries with others is also important, but you don't want these boundaries to box you in either. Work on creating boundaries by standing up for yourself, staying true to yourself, but also learning how to love, even if it has to be from a distance.

♄♏︎
SATURN IN SCORPIO
OR EIGHTH HOUSE

KARMIC LESSON trusting your inner knowing

Part of your karmic lessons in this life is learning how to keep evolving and embracing the changes that come your way as you move through your life. You are working through your fear of change and your fear of things transitioning and moving forward. Even though things may be removed or cleared from your life, there is always something new coming in to take its place. Trusting this process and allowing yourself to move through the changes and transitions that come your way can lead to a new power and can help you step into a more confident and aligned place.

Surrendering to the dark unknown that often comes along with change is where your creative powers lie. This is how you can keep reinventing yourself and moving to higher levels of awareness and consciousness. Life is meant to be experienced, so don't get stuck where you are. Acknowledge the fear, but also know that amazing things can happen when you take a leap of faith and allow your life to transform.

♄♐
SATURN IN SAGITTARIUS
OR NINTH HOUSE

KARMIC LESSON expanding what you already know

You want to run free with the wind, but life has other plans and responsibilities that crop up to hold you back. You are being asked to take a slower and more methodical approach to your life, and to think carefully before acting. There is some wisdom in learning how to set boundaries and follow the rules. Eventually, this way of living can get a little, well, boring. If you don't give your desire for freedom an outlet, you are going to encounter this boredom and perhaps also feel angry or disgruntled with the direction of your life. Yes, you have responsibilities that need attending to that are difficult to escape, but you also have to make the time to focus on joy and play.

There is a bright spark of optimism in you. Don't let it flicker away because you feel the heavy weight of responsibility creeping in. There is a power and a strength in learning to step up and take charge of your life. There is a strength that comes when you choose to own your life and the journey you are taking.

♄♑
SATURN IN CAPRICORN
OR TENTH HOUSE

KARMIC LESSON redefining success

You are logical, hardworking, and driven by your ambitions. Through the first part of your life you may crave discipline and flourish when you are given clear guidance and boundaries. Eventually you will have to find a balance between working hard and learning to lighten up. Your lesson in this life is learning to enjoy the process. Set your sights not on your destination but in each and every moment that has been given to you. Learn to balance your energy levels and not burn yourself out chasing success. You need to give yourself boundaries when it comes to your work ethic, your ambitions, and your definition of success. You also need to learn to not be so hard on yourself and others, and to embrace the softer and gentler sides of your personality. Goals and ambitions are far more rewarding when they spark joy.

♄♒
SATURN IN AQUARIUS
OR ELEVENTH HOUSE

KARMIC LESSON listening to your own needs

Part of your karmic lessons in this life is learning to separate yourself from those around you. Rather than rely on those around you, you need to learn to rely on yourself and find a way to be self-sufficient, even when you are in a committed relationship.

Saturn in Aquarius also indicates that part of your purpose is to bring a higher vision to the world. You have a big heart, and while this can land you in codependent relationships, it can also inspire a new way of doing things and a new way to think about how humanity can best be served. Your big heart coupled with your great organizational skills can see you do a lot of good in your community and for the world at large. You can be an angel for others and have the power and potential to bring more love, healing, and support to the world.

♄♓
SATURN IN PISCES
OR TWELFTH HOUSE

KARMIC LESSON balancing discipline and creativity

Your creative innovations and designs are a gift to this world, so don't hold yourself back from sharing your creativity, in whatever form it comes to you. Part of your karmic lessons in this life is learning to take this incredible creativity that you have and bring some discipline or grounded energy to it. Along with your amazing creative talents, you are also deeply spiritual and may feel that you have walked this Earth many times before. You have a deep wisdom inside of you and an innate understanding of spirituality. Having a grounded spiritual practice can help you create a sense of balance and dive deeper into your inner knowing. You are in the physical world, so don't get lost in your mind or in the spirit realms. You are a soul with a physical body for a reason, and it is up to you to embrace and find that reason.

Planets of Higher Consciousness

URANUS   NEPTUNE   PLUTO

The planets of higher consciousness are Uranus, Neptune, and Pluto. These planets work with us on a subconscious level, which means we don't notice their lessons and gifts unless we are paying attention. As these planets work quietly in the background of our lives, it is often only once they are done that we are able to see the journey of transformation we have gone through. As these planets take years to orbit the Sun, their effects can also be seen on a global or generational level.

11

Uranus

ZODIAC RULER Aquarius

KEYWORDS innovation, surprise, change, upheaval, rebellion, freedom

RULES OVER science, futuristic technology, artificial intelligence, humanitarianism, natural disasters, astrology, kundalini/spiritual awakenings

Has anything ever happened to you that took you by complete surprise and radically changed and shifted your whole world overnight? That was likely the work of Uranus. Uranus is known as the great awakener for its energy that brings radical change—the change that causes revolution and upheaval to pave the way for a brighter future. Uranus awakens us to a new truth and a new power by breaking us free from the things that are no longer serving us and the things that no longer support our highest growth.

Uranus also represents modern innovation, entrepreneurship, and forward thinking. Uranus is the radical, the revolutionary that is always pushing boundaries and helping us get out of our comfort zone. Uranus wants to break down walls and remove boundaries. It wants us to find our freedom from labels and from judgments, and to see each other as one. Uranus also rules the advancement of technology. Its energy inspires us to keep dreaming up inventive ways that technology can change the world and integrate into our lives.

♅♈
URANUS IN ARIES
OR FIRST HOUSE

GENERATIONAL LESSON to break the status quo and long-standing traditions and find new ways of doing things

You are a headstrong, passionate, and fiery soul that has come here to pave a new path forward, one that has never been done before. While your mind is full of ingenious ideas, you may also get carried away and be unable to focus on the task at hand. You may have plenty of ideas, but lack the groundedness and the focus to actually execute them.

Your fiery nature can also be your own worst enemy. It can help drive your purpose and your passions, but it can also cause your temper to flare and make you hold on to resentments and betrayal. Keeping these things close to your heart will never serve you, so rather than plotting an elaborate way to get revenge, it is better to release it, bring acceptance to it, and work on forgiveness.

The dates for Uranus through the signs may overlap due to its retrograde movements.

♅♈

URANUS IN TAURUS
OR SECOND HOUSE

GENERATIONAL LESSON to focus on healing the planet
and looking after the resources we have been given

You are a builder, and part of your purpose in this life is to take your creative and inventive ideas and turn them into realities. You have the gift of taking creative ideas and inspirations and bringing them to life in a real and tangible way. While this steady and methodical approach helps you make leaps and bounds, it is also important that you allow yourself to be flexible and adaptable to any road bumps. When you get stuck in one area of your life for too long, or too fixated on your plans, it's most likely a sign that the time has come to pivot or let go. Acknowledge what holds you back or what you are clinging to, and then allow yourself to break free so you can move forward. While you crave stability, no growth can come from remaining in your comfort zone forever.

⛢♊
URANUS IN GEMINI
OR THIRD HOUSE

GENERATIONAL LESSON to keep an open mind and
to bring people together using technology

You have sharp intuition and a knack for picking up on subtle clues in your environment and in people. All of this makes you highly attractive and charming, and perhaps people feel like they know you after just having met you. You can also adapt to whatever situation you find yourself in, which can come in handy, but it can also be used to manipulate and take advantage of others. Be mindful if you find yourself doing this.

You are a student of life, and everyone you meet has some wisdom to impart. Keep an open mind and always be open to learning new things; when you do, you will find that you can thrive. It is often through the connections you build and the relationships you create that you can find your way to your path and purpose.

⛢♈
URANUS IN CANCER
OR FOURTH HOUSE

GENERATIONAL LESSON to bring change to family dynamics
and the way people choose to live

Part of your purpose in this life is learning how to radically accept yourself and your past, and then to take that radical acceptance and use it to shine your light and go for your goals.

Wholeheartedly accepting who you are allows you to feel strong and confident to go after what you want, and to bring your creative ideas and visions to the table. Be mindful of when you find yourself playing small or when you shrink back to fit in or be agreeable. You are your strongest when you can own all of who you are, so keep showing up in your truth.

Keep shining your light and moving from your heart. You have a strong heart energy field, so tune in to the wisdom of your heart when you are feeling stuck. With a sensitive heart, you need to give yourself time to recharge your batteries and ground yourself before heading back into the world with your heart on your sleeve.

⛢♈
URANUS IN LEO
OR FIFTH HOUSE

GENERATIONAL LESSON to bring change to how
we choose to lead and guide people

You have bold ideas and a clear vision for how you can create a brighter future. When you feel passionate about something, when you follow the beat of your heart, there is little you cannot achieve. However, you need to be mindful of allowing your pride and ego to get in the way. Learn to work as a team and collaborate with your efforts rather than dominate. Part of your purpose in this life is stepping into your role as a leader. To be a good leader, you have to aim toward unity and understanding, rather than trying to tell people what to do. You are also highly creative, and when you tune in and connect with this creativity, you will always be able to find solutions to your problems.

⽩♈

URANUS IN VIRGO
OR SIXTH HOUSE

GENERATIONAL LESSON to find our strength and independence

You have the mind of a seeker and are always looking for new experiences. Your aim is often to perfect things or to perfect life. You want to try it all before settling on your decision. Part of your purpose in this life is learning how to get out of your head and into the spontaneity of your heart. Sometimes you will not have access to all the information needed to make the best and most perfect decision, and that is okay. The more you trust yourself and your intuition, the easier it will be for you to make those decisions when you find yourself at a fork in the road.

Along with trusting your intuition, claiming your independence is also a source of power. You need to tune in to that part of you that may not always have the answers, but has the strength and the determination to make it through no matter what life brings your way.

⽩♈

URANUS IN LIBRA
OR SEVENTH HOUSE

GENERATIONAL LESSON to work for equality
and freedom, especially in partnerships

You are here to explore and grow through the people you surround yourself with. You may find yourself drawn to an eclectic group of people. Having a sense of freedom is important to you, especially when it comes to the person you choose to partner with. You may also long for creative freedom in the workplace.

You have the natural gift of seeing things from a balanced and fair state of mind. This ability can make you empathetic, and you are a person many people trust or feel safe confiding in.

While you do long for freedom, you are extremely loyal and can often tell when someone is lying or trying to deceive you. In fact, you are a good judge of character and have a strong intuition when someone or something is not right. You may also feel yourself absorbing or taking on the emotions of others. If this ever gets overwhelming, be sure to come back to your center and work on grounding yourself and your energy. As you move through your soul journey, you are likely to have a positive and even life-changing effect on those around you.

♅♈︎
URANUS IN SCORPIO
OR EIGHTH HOUSE

GENERATIONAL LESSON   to bring change to how we choose
to understand ourselves, our traumas, and our emotions

You are always seeking to better understand yourself and the deeper meaning behind what you are feeling or experiencing. When you learn to go within and unpack your traumas or those uncomfortable emotions, a great breakthrough can occur. Part of your purpose in this life is learning to take a journey of self-inquiry and to keep doing the work to understand yourself on a deeper level. Through this understanding, you can unlock new potentials and push yourself further in life. Know as you go within and bring a sense of acceptance to who you are that you can make leaps and bounds in this life and attract more of what you desire.

⛢♐

URANUS IN SAGITTARIUS
OR NINTH HOUSE

GENERATIONAL LESSON to change how we view ourselves
spiritually and our higher purpose for living

You crave freedom when it comes to going after your purpose and doing what will fulfill you and make you happy. You are not content doing something for the sake of doing it; it has to have meaning for you. If you ever feel stagnant or stuck, look to your goals and what you are pursuing: Is the purpose still there? If not, it may be time for a change or to restructure a particular area of your life. Our dreams grow and change as we do.

You are a seeker of truth, but this seeking can get you into trouble because very often, everyone has their own version of the truth. While you may want people to see things your way, that is not always going to be the case, and there may be harsh lessons for you if you try to move through your life with this mindset. It is far more powerful for you to enter a place where you are free and brave enough to seek your personal truths.

⛢♈

URANUS IN CAPRICORN
OR TENTH HOUSE

GENERATIONAL LESSON to overhaul and bring change
to traditional or "tried and true" establishments

You have a natural ability to take what has been tested and proven and add to it to make it better or make it your own.

You can bring innovation to long-standing traditions and create new meaning from them. In a sense, you can find this perfect balance between respecting and honoring traditions and making them more relevant to the world we live in today. When you use this approach, you can excel, especially with your career and in matters of business. You have a natural authority and power, and when you use this in a productive way, you can easily win over respect and get things done.

♅♈
URANUS IN AQUARIUS
OR ELEVENTH HOUSE

GENERATIONAL LESSON to bring change and radical advancements to technology and to take part in creating a society built on equality

You are an innovator and may find you are naturally gifted and drawn to technology. You have an entrepreneurial soul, and you have the natural ability to find ways to do things in a more effective and automated manner. You crave freedom, like to make your own rules, and do things to the beat of your own drum. You may also feel driven to support humanitarian causes and to focus on building a world that is more fair, just, and equal.

♅♈
URANUS IN PISCES
OR TWELFTH HOUSE

GENERATIONAL LESSON to recognize the oneness in each other
and to hold the vision of creating a beautiful and better world

Uranus in Pisces is dreamy, creative, and loves nothing more
than to escape from reality. You may find yourself drawn to
fantasy worlds or deep diving into your spiritual journey. It is
part of your purpose in this life to share your creative visions
and sparks with the world around you. The more you can shine
in your true unique essence, the easier this will be. In times of
stress, you may also benefit from taking time to rest, recharge,
and lose yourself in something that brings you joy and fills you
up. Uranus in Pisces is about escaping this physical earthly
dimension and diving into other realms; we just have to
remember to keep ourselves grounded as we allow our imaginations to soar.

12

Neptune

ZODIAC RULER Pisces

KEYWORDS illusions, dreams, confusion, creativity

RULES OVER dreams, intuition, visual arts/photography, entertainment industry, movies, theater, magic, alcohol/drugs/escapism

Neptune is the planet of dreams, illusions, and higher consciousness. It is creative, artistic, and loves to escape reality. Neptune is also believed to be a gateway to higher realms and the home of unconditional love. When its energy shines down on the planet and in our own lives, we are reminded that we are all connected and our souls are all from the same family. No matter our differences, Neptune reminds us that we are more similar than we realize and more connected than we will ever know.

Neptune moves slowly, taking 165 years to orbit the Sun. It also spends up to fourteen years in a particular zodiac sign. For this reason, the sign your Neptune is in at the time of your birth indicates your generational lessons. For more of a personal look, you will want to pay extra attention to the house placement.

· ·

♆♈
NEPTUNE IN ARIES
OR FIRST HOUSE

GENERATIONAL LESSON to become the hero of your own life

Neptune in Aries is the hero coming to save us from our troubles. This hero promises to take away all of our pain and suffering and to make things right again. Like all things Neptunian, the illusion eventually fades and we are left feeling manipulated and taken advantage of.

Neptune in Aries may paint the picture of needing a hero to swoop in and save us, but this is the illusion. In truth, the only person who can save us is ourselves. Sure, we can reach out to others for support and guidance, but no one else can step in and make the changes that are needed.

For many of us, the true hero we are waiting for lives within us. We have the power to make the changes and take the steps needed to create the life we desire. No one else knows what it's like to walk in our shoes; no one else knows what calls to our soul except ourselves. Stepping up to be the champion and hero of your own life is the message when Neptune is in Aries.

♆♉
NEPTUNE IN TAURUS
OR SECOND HOUSE

GENERATIONAL LESSON to find abundance by working in unity with nature and all of life

With Neptune in Taurus, it is important we connect to the Earth and remember it is a precious resource that must be loved and not abused. On one level, Neptune in Taurus can make us greedy and can lead to the abuse of natural resources. But once the Neptune veil has been removed, we can see that our ways of greed are not only unsustainable, but not as fulfilling as they promised to be.

With Neptune in Taurus, the call is to work in harmony with the cycles of the Earth. Rather than taking, we are asked to work with nature and tune in to the abundance it is offering us. When we learn to work with its rhythms, we find there is always enough and there is always plenty for all. Neptune in Taurus calls for us to balance the scales and create more equality, especially when it comes to the way the planet's resources are being used.

♆♊
NEPTUNE IN GEMINI
OR THIRD HOUSE

GENERATIONAL LESSON to balance the mind and the soul, and to have the two working in harmony

Neptune in Gemini is the wise old sage sitting atop the mountain. From down below, it looks like the sage knows it all. But upon taking the treacherous trek up the mountain, you realize you didn't need to be there in the first place. The trek has taught you everything you need to know. From the top of the mountain, your problems look so much smaller—but this has nothing to do with the sage and everything to do with your perspective.

As you took the trek to the top of the mountain, you had to wrestle with your body, mind, and soul. All three working together is often how we find the solutions to our problems and navigate through our lives. With Neptune in Gemini, we are called to take a mind, body, and soul approach to our lives. The Gemini twins want us to build that bridge between the heavens and the earth, and Neptune's presence simply amplifies that. By balancing our inner world, we find balance in our outer world.

♆ ♋
NEPTUNE IN CANCER
OR FOURTH HOUSE

GENERATIONAL LESSON to follow our hearts and build supportive family

With Neptune in Cancer, our heart field energy is amplified and it is easier to tune in to its wisdom and potential. We may also feel more compassionate toward one another or more focused on creating loving and supportive communities and families.

While our heart carries its own wisdom, we cannot ignore the wisdom of our mind in the process. Sometimes our heart knows the way, but sometimes we also need the grounding and structure that comes from our rational and logical mind. Neptune in Cancer challenges us to balance these dynamics and learn when to follow our heart and when we need to ground ourselves. Neptune in Cancer can also stir the desire to create and honor family values. We may feel a push toward creating a more supportive family environment or, alternatively, working to create clearer and more balanced boundaries with our family.

♆ ♌
NEPTUNE IN LEO
OR FIFTH HOUSE

Neptune in Leo wants to be adored, loved, cherished, and praised. It has incredible artistic talents too. Neptune in Leo is definitely a creative force we can all take and use in our lives. We also have to remember our creative efforts, and what we put into the world is not a measure of our value or worth.

Receiving admiration and praise is a human need, but as we get older, we tend to fall into a trap when we look for or even chase external praise. When we want those around us to love and admire us, we tend to lose our way, and act not from a place of truth but from a place of trying to please. Over time, this throws us out of our natural alignment and takes us away from our true selves. True alignment and power come when we learn to praise and ultimately love ourselves. While we can search for love from others, we cannot appreciate it to its fullest until we have learned to wholeheartedly love ourselves. When you are taking your final breaths on this planet, the thing that matters is how you feel about yourself and not what others think of you. And in those final moments, you deserve to be loving yourself and the life you've led.

♆ ♍
NEPTUNE IN VIRGO
OR SIXTH HOUSE

GENERATIONAL LESSON to find the sacred in the mundane

Neptune in Virgo wants us to find the spiritual in the everyday. How often have you found yourself doing a mundane task and drifting off into another world? Before you know it, all this time has passed and you wonder where you have been! During moments like this, without realizing it, you have entered a meditative state. Taking that sensation and applying it in a more mindful way is all meditation is. Even the most banal tasks can become sacred when we allow them to be. With Neptune in Virgo, we can be drawn to and reminded of this, and we may even reach new states of enlightenment when we embrace this mindset.

♆ ♎
NEPTUNE IN LIBRA
OR SEVENTH HOUSE

GENERATIONAL LESSON to reexamine justice and what is fair

Libra is the sign of justice and fairness, but Neptune can cloud the waters. What is really fair? And is doing the fair thing always the right thing to do? With Neptune in Libra, the water can get muddy and our judgment can be clouded. This is only so we can stretch our minds and imaginations and reconsider what we deem as fair and what we deem as right, and when it's acceptable or not for these two ideas to cross over.

Neptune in Libra is also sensitive and creative. It can bring new fashion or design trends, and often those with Neptune in Libra have a style and elegance to them. Having style and elegance is not so much about what you are wearing but more how you choose to carry yourself.

♆ ♏
NEPTUNE IN SCORPIO
OR EIGHTH HOUSE

GENERATIONAL LESSON to shift darkness into light

With Neptune in Scorpio, you may have a strong desire to understand your emotions and your subconscious mind. It's not enough for you to live on the surface; you long to dive deep and to keep peeling back the layers until you find whatever it is that you are looking for. Neptune in Scorpio is also a sensitive and psychic placement, and you may feel your intuition strongly in your gut. Listen and trust your intuition, and follow through on its wisdom.

Scorpio also rules over divination, so you may feel drawn to working in or exploring this field. If you have ever been curious, buy a deck of tarot cards or pull up the natal chart of your friend and give your friend a reading—you may as well take advantage of these natural abilities that have been given to you!

♆♐
NEPTUNE IN SAGITTARIUS
OR NINTH HOUSE

GENERATIONAL LESSON to open people's minds to radical new ideas

Neptune in Sagittarius is big and expansive, and it opens your heart and mind to new possibilities and new ways of thinking about things. There is a desire to break free from the traditions of our past or our culture and to find a new and more modern way of doing things.

Neptune in Sagittarius favors learning by experience. It makes you spontaneous and a little adventurous, and it also gives you a fierce streak of independence. You are not afraid to share your opinions and to let others know what you are thinking and feeling. As Neptune can create some fogginess, you may at times find yourself out of touch with those around you or blinded as to how your words may make others feel. You need to work on keeping yourself grounded and finding ways to express yourself that are thoughtful but still allow you to stay true to yourself.

♆♑
NEPTUNE IN CAPRICORN
OR TENTH HOUSE

GENERATIONAL LESSON to turn dreams into tangible realities

Neptune in Capricorn is about finding your center among the flow. Your gifts and talents in this life rest in keeping your cool and staying grounded, even as life is ebbing and flowing around you. Your generation is here to remind us all that our center and our state of balance are not about what is happening around us but what is happening inside of us.

Neptune in Capricorn is powerful for manifestation. The dreamy quality of Neptune allows our imagination to soar, while the practical Capricorn helps us put pen to paper to get things done. With Neptune in Capricorn, there is no dream too big and no ambition too great. Get your dreams and ideas onto paper, and write down what you would like to create and achieve. Go big with it, and allow your imagination to take hold. Then, look back over what you wrote and see if you can make a bullet list of actions you can take to turn your dream into a reality.

♆♒
NEPTUNE IN AQUARIUS
OR ELEVENTH HOUSE

GENERATIONAL LESSON to inspire independent thinking
and changes that benefit all

Neptune in Aquarius brings radical innovation and thinking outside of the box. There is also a strong push toward humanitarian efforts and bringing people together to build stronger and more sustainable communities. Your ideas are supposed to be big and bold, so don't censor yourself just because those around you don't understand. You want to be open to feedback, but part of your purpose in this life is to switch things on their head and to think about things in a new way.

Along with having many bright ideas, you are a humanitarian at heart. In fact, part of your purpose and passion in this life stems from helping and being of service to others. When you are feeling stressed or anxious, one of the best remedies for you is to put your own problems to the side for a moment and go help someone else.

♆ ♓
NEPTUNE IN PISCES
OR TWELFTH HOUSE

GENERATIONAL LESSON to let go of the ego
and finding our spiritual connection

Neptune in Pisces is about dissolving the ego to make way for the spirit to shine through. When we become aware of our egocentric habits, like living from a scarcity mindset, feeling the need to compete with others, feeling superior or less than others, or being in a judgmental headspace, we are able to transcend them and shift past limited beliefs into something more loving and unifying.

Learning to create healthy boundaries is important with Neptune in Pisces. Because the energy can be so unconditional and loving, we want to make sure we are also taking the measures needed to protect ourselves. It is perfectly okay to love from a distance, and it is perfectly okay to love someone and not want them in your life. Neptune in Pisces is also highly creative and can bring advancements to creative industries, in particular to the music industry, seeing as Pisces rules over music.

13

⚳

Pluto

ZODIAC RULER Scorpio

KEYWORDS death/rebirth, transformation, metamorphosis,
shadow work, power, underworld, obsession

RULES OVER power positions, great wealth, dictatorships,
abuse, secrets, higher consciousness, detoxing

Pluto is the planet of death and rebirth. Its energy governs the process of the phoenix rising from the ashes. At first, something needs to burn and die, and from these ashes, a rebirth is possible that allows us to tune in to a greater power than before. As Pluto moves so slowly, the sign it falls in is more generational than personal. The house placement will be more personal, as it indicates where you will express this energy.

PLUTO: LORD OF THE UNDERWORLD

Pluto is considered the Lord of the Underworld, and it is about digging through our shadows and the darker, deeper stuff to transform it into light. Pluto is a little dark and mysterious, and when its energy is highlighted in our chart or in the sky, it often signals we are about to go through a transformation.

Pluto moves the slowest of all the planets, taking 248 years to orbit the Sun. This makes Pluto's movements even more powerful as they are so long lasting. It also means that some people will experience Plutonian energy more than others.

Look to where Pluto is in the sky right now and then match its location in your chart. For example, if Pluto is currently at 1 degree of Aquarius, look to where 1 degree of Aquarius falls in your chart.

If Pluto is within a few degrees of your ascendant, descendant, nadir, or any of your natal planets, that area of your life will be under Pluto's spell of transformation.

If you do have Pluto crossing a sensitive point in your chart or aligning with your Sun or Moon, know that it is pretty special! It also indicates that your soul signed up for a big transformation in this life and wanted to move into a new and higher vibration.

Pluto's transformational work usually takes about a decade to complete because it moves so slowly, but sometimes it can bring obvious and clear shifts into our lives. When Pluto is around, something has to be burned away. There has to be some destruction of life as we once knew it in order to pave a new way.

Pluto's transformation can be painful and challenging. There is often a type of death involved that can lead to feelings of grief, confusion, and despair. Pluto can feel dark and a little depressing, and it can be hard to see the light at the end of the tunnel.

This constant cycle of life and death that we see in nature reminds us that just like the leaves, we have to learn how to let go and surrender to the ebbs and flows and changes that life brings. They are always temporary, and every state we find ourselves in will pass. When you are going through a difficult transformation or if you notice Pluto moving into a prominent place in your chart, allow nature to be your guide and recognize that just like the phoenix, you will rise from the ashes with bigger wings and a brighter inner fire.

♇ ♈
PLUTO IN ARIES
OR FIRST HOUSE

GENERATIONAL LESSON Who am I?

The Lord of the Underworld in the sign of the warrior helps us claim our power and remember that true power comes when we allow our independent spirit to shine. When we honor our unique spark and feel confident in who we are, there is no limit to what we can achieve or how far we can rise.

Pluto in Aries is fiery, passionate, and wants to keep transforming to discover new adventures and new limits of its potential. This can also be a destructive combination, as Pluto in Aries is not afraid to make things burn big and bright to bring about the change it is looking for. You are not afraid to explore things on a deeper level, and there is a good chance that your soul signed up for a life of transformation. You have a strong desire to keep peeling back the layers and revealing new dimensions and truths from inside of yourself.

Pluto in the first house can also indicate that you are destined to go through a transformative life experience that will bring lasting change.

♀♉
PLUTO IN TAURUS
OR SECOND HOUSE

GENERATIONAL LESSON What am I holding onto?

The Lord of the Underworld in the sign of the methodical and practical bull is not always the best fit. Pluto wants to transform, to set things alight, and watch them burn so something new can take its place. Taurus wants to control and take its time figuring out what needs to go and what needs to stay.

Pluto dominates here, so it is best to surrender to the flow and allow whatever needs to go to go, without feeling the need to hold on. The more we attach and try to grasp at things, the more stressed we become, and we are less likely to recognize the new opportunities when they arise. Sometimes we attach ourselves to things or ideas because we think they will make us feel better or because they give us a sense of identity. No "thing" or belief is really who we truly are.

Taurus wants us to hold on to things because it brings a sense of comfort and stability. Pluto reminds us that sometimes we have to be on unstable ground to transform and push ourselves to the next level. When you discover the truth of who you are and learn to stand in your power, it will be easier for you to trust the flow of what leaves and enters your life.

♀♊
PLUTO IN GEMINI
OR THIRD HOUSE

GENERATIONAL LESSON How do I express myself?

When Pluto is in Gemini, our mind undergoes a transformation, shifting and changing, so it can reach new levels of understanding, communication, and compassion.

With our mind transformed, we can get to work on taking new actions in our physical lives. Pluto in Gemini takes on two personas: one helps us change things from an internal level and the other helps us change things on an external level. Very often, it's the internal shift that has to come first. As we change our perspective and learn to look at things differently, the things we are looking at tend to change.

You have the power when it comes to your voice and the messages you have to share with the world. When you speak, people tend to listen, so use your gifts of communication to get your ideas and thoughts into the world.

♇ ♋
PLUTO IN CANCER
OR FOURTH HOUSE

GENERATIONAL LESSON What does family mean to me?

The Lord of the Underworld in the sign of the crab allows us to feel our emotions deeply. Our sensitivity is heightened, and we are able to become more aware of our energetic body or our life force energy. Our psychic abilities or intuition can also be heightened with this placement.

With Pluto in Cancer, there is a strong instinct to protect and stand up for things that matter to you. You may feel a strong sense of allyship when it comes to your family, culture, or ancestry. Your family life is at the heart of any transformations you undertake. You need to be extra mindful of giving away your identity to family structures or rules, or to the wants and desires of the world around you. You may feel like you are losing yourself at times, but by standing up for yourself and going after the things you love and desire, you are able to claim more of your personal power.

♇♌
PLUTO IN LEO
OR FIFTH HOUSE

GENERATIONAL LESSON What is love?

With Pluto in Leo, we may find ourselves continually having to transform and change our lives when we are led by our ego rather than our heart. Pluto in Leo can create a sense that all that glitters isn't gold. We may find ourselves swept up by someone or something we desire, only to find out it's not what was promised or that the rug was pulled out from under us at the last second. These lessons cannot be avoided sometimes, but this is when you are called to transform and make decisions from a place of heartfelt truth rather than your ego. The ego likes you to believe that you need more in order to be happy and satisfied. The heart knows that true happiness and satisfaction have nothing to do with your external reality and everything to do with your internal one.

Your relationships can be highly transformative and revealing for you. It is through your relationships, especially romantic ones, that you are able to discover more of who you are and what love means to you.

♇♍
PLUTO IN VIRGO
OR SIXTH HOUSE

GENERATIONAL LESSON What makes me worthy?

The Lord of the Underworld in the sign of the independent virgin is about taking back and claiming your personal power. It is about recognizing how strong you are and not letting your goals, dreams, and desires fall by the wayside to please or appease others.

With Pluto in Virgo, there may be some transformation to go through in regard to this. You may find that you have to give things up to discover your true independence again, or you may find that life removes things from your path so you can step into your full independence. Being independent is not about being alone or doing things on your own; it is about finding the strength and resilience you need to create the best and most fulfilling life for you, regardless of your circumstances.

Pluto in the sixth house especially can indicate a strong mind–body connection. When you are feeling something on a mental level, you tend to notice it showing up on a physical level, so it's important to keep your stress levels under control.

♇ ♎

PLUTO IN LIBRA
OR SEVENTH HOUSE

GENERATIONAL LESSON What do I stand for?

The Lord of the Underworld in the sign of the scales is about transforming things to create more balance. When the scales get tipped in one direction over the other, Pluto begins weaving its magic and reminding us of the importance of keeping things in balance.

Sometimes we have to be pushed to extremes to find our middle ground. Pluto in Libra is pushing boundaries and helping us find a new center. Just when we think we have it all figured out, we are challenged and pushed yet again to find a new truth. Life is a constant process of losing yourself only to find yourself again. Embrace the unknown and the uncertainty when it arises, and know that these are points in your life when you are doing the most growing.

Pluto in the seventh house can indicate a marriage or partnership that is deeply transformative.

♀♏
PLUTO IN SCORPIO
OR EIGHTH HOUSE

GENERATIONAL LESSON What does it mean to die?

Pluto is ruled by Scorpio, so the Lord of the Underworld feels most at home in the sign of the scorpion. The scorpion itself is a symbol for change and transformation. When the scorpion sheds its skin, it is at its most vulnerable and the process can be stressful. Then it's very delicate for a few days as its shell becomes hard again. When we go through our own metamorphosis, we, too, may feel vulnerable and stressed. We may wish to go into hiding and feel the need to hold ourselves back and make ourselves small. But eventually, our outer shell toughens once again.

With Pluto in Scorpio, transformation is the name of the game. You came into this life to keep shedding your skin and reinventing yourself as you move through your life journey. You are not likely to go through one significant metamorphosis, but several. You are always in the process of peeling back layers and looking to understand yourself on deeper levels. The surface level doesn't interest you; you crave deeper connections with yourself, others, and the world. Pluto in the eighth house can also indicate psychic and intuitive gifts.

♀♐
PLUTO IN SAGITTARIUS
OR NINTH HOUSE

GENERATIONAL LESSON What is freedom?

The Lord of the Underworld in Sagittarius is about transforming to find a greater freedom. This sense of freedom can come on a mental level through an expansion of ideas and beliefs, especially

It's a rare combination, but having Pluto and Sagittarius's ruler, Jupiter, conjunct or within 5 to 7 degrees of each other in your natal chart is known as the millionaire's aspect and can indicate great wealth and prosperity.

through higher education. It can also manifest on a physical level through traveling to far-off destinations or finding the freedom to go after your own dreams and goals. You seek a deeper meaning when it comes to life. You don't want to skim the surface; you want to dive in and understand things on all levels of your being.

With Pluto in Sagittarius, there are no boundaries or limits on what you can achieve in this life, and there is a sense that life is an adventure that is meant to be explored. You don't want to commit to one thing; you want to be able to taste and experience all of what life has to offer. Allowing yourself to explore helps take you to new levels of consciousness. Allowing your mind to expand to new dimensions helps you find a greater freedom and a deeper sense of truth of who you truly are.

♀ ♑
PLUTO IN CAPRICORN
OR TENTH HOUSE

GENERATIONAL LESSON What is true power?

The Lord of the Underworld in the sign of the sea goat is about transforming the rules and regulations we have chosen to live by. The way things were done that could be seen as standard, traditional, and tried and true are all up for review so progress can be made.

Pluto in Capricorn indicates you like to shake up the status quo and get people to think differently about why they are choosing to do things. It is about taking responsibility for the changes we wish to see in our own lives, rather than waiting for others to make the changes for us.

Pluto in the tenth house can indicate great power and success when it comes to your career.

♇ ≈

PLUTO IN AQUARIUS
OR ELEVENTH HOUSE

GENERATIONAL LESSON How am I connected?

With Pluto in Aquarius, there is a focus on finding ways to support the whole community rather than just the individual. There is a desire to transform the world through focusing on strengthening communities.

Pluto in Aquarius indicates transformation when it comes to the structure and framework of society. It indicates changes in how we come together to support ourselves and each other. Pluto in Aquarius can also bring changes to humanitarian efforts and how we approach the giving and spending of resources. The psychic energy of both Pluto and Aquarius also merge to bring deeply spiritual and profound experiences that can lead to healing.

Pluto in the eleventh house can indicate a karmic friendship or a platonic soul mate connection that you are destined to experience in this life.

♀♓
PLUTO IN PISCES
OR TWELFTH HOUSE

GENERATIONAL LESSON What is real and what is illusion?

This is a magical and mystical placement. We are likely to see the uncovering of some deep, dark secrets that can lead to revelations and transformations. There may be a shift to a more spiritual way of life.

Pluto in Pisces can also bring advancements in how we understand the way our mind works. There are opportunities here for deep and lasting transformation through the discoveries that are made, and perhaps we will never be able to think about ourselves or our existence in the same way again.

Pluto in the twelfth house can indicate skeletons that need to be unearthed from your closet, not just from this life but from previous lifetimes too. Even though this work can be tiring, it is well worth it. As you keep digging and facing your fears and confronting the things that keep you up at night, you are returning to a new power and a new strength. This is also a very psychic placement, indicating gifts of mediumship.

RESOURCES

Visit **foreverconscious.com** for the latest intuitive astrology updates, including monthly forecasts, moon rituals, and more.

HOW TO DRAW YOUR BIRTH CHART

There are so many free online tools that will draw up a free natal birth chart for you. Check out astro.com, astro-charts.com, or alabe.com for some good options.

HOW TO FIND THE CURRENT
TROPICAL POSITIONS OF THE PLANETS

Locating the current position of the planets can be done using an Ephemeris. You can find them online or in book format. A popular book is *The New American Ephemeris*. You can also use any of the astrology software/apps listed below.

ASTROLOGY SOFTWARE/APPS

Time Passages and Solar Fire are great for birth charts, keeping track of the planets, and drawing more advanced charts.

ACKNOWLEDGMENTS

In gratitude to all the astrologers who came before me—the ones whose blogs I read, whose books I borrowed from the library, and whose videos I watched on this journey of learning the art and magic of the stars. Thank you to Jill Alexander and the team at Quarto and Fair Winds Press, the wonderful editor, Jenna Nelson Patton, and literary agent, Giles Anderson. And finally, a big, heartfelt thank you to all the readers of foreverconscious.com: Your enthusiasm to keep learning and your words of encouragement have guided me further on my journey of decoding the stars. This book would not be possible without all of you.

ABOUT THE AUTHOR

TANAAZ CHUBB is an intuitive writer and creator of foreverconscious.com—one of the largest astrology and spiritual blogs on the Internet. From a young age, Tanaaz felt very connected to the spirit world, and much of her writing comes from her connection with the Divine. She has written the books *The Power of Positive Energy, Messages for the Soul*, and *My Pocket Mantras*. Tanaaz hopes that her writings will empower, uplift, and inspire readers from all over the world. She was born and raised in Melbourne, Australia, but now lives in Los Angeles with her husband and Maltipoo. You can follow her on all major social media platforms under @ForeverConscious.

INDEX